Discovery—

The Art of Leading Small Groups

Discovery—
The Art of Leading Small Groups

with supplement
A Bible Study Guide on Ephesians

by
Marion K. Rich

Beacon Hill Press of Kansas City
Kansas City, Missouri

Permission to quote from the following copyrighted versions of the Bible
is acknowledged with appreciation:

Good News Bible, Today's English Version (TEV). Old Testament ©
American Bible Society, 1976; New Testament © American Bible
Society, 1966, 1971, 1976.

New International Version of the New Testament (NIV), © 1973 by the
New York Bible Society International.

Dedication

Affectionately dedicated to a group of wonderful women who continually radiate a love of Christ by their faithfulness, their committed lives, their concern for others, and their never-failing cheerfulness—the ladies' prayer fellowship of Kansas City Metropolitan Church of the Nazarene.

Contents

Preface

My first encounter with a small, spiritual group came many years ago as a teenager. I was playing basketball in my high school gymnasium and the girl who was my guard was a Christian. She was friendly. She had a sense of humor. She was interested in me. At the close of the game, Dorothy Jones, my guard, invited me to a young people's prayer fellowship in a home.

I had never been in such a group before. The gang I had run around with were quite wild—interested only in parties, dancing, and driving around in cars. This new group of young people had a different kind of joy—a fullness to life—a quality of honesty—an openness that makes one eager to face himself and his problems. I was impressed!

They sang songs and lively choruses that were new to me. They shared God's love and told of their vital relationship to Him. Then they prayed. I had never heard anyone pray aloud before except for memorized prayers. These prayers were honest expressions of needs and requests. There were indications of real concerns and heart burdens for others who did not know Christ. These were young people praying. They were speaking directly to God—simply, honestly, just as we talk to one in whom we have real confidence. I wished I too could pray like that.

After the prayer time there were refreshments and fellowship and a time of making new friends. They invited me to return to their group the next Tuesday evening at another home. I felt accepted and loved.

All week I thought about the prayer group. All week I wished I too could pray audibly. As the week progressed the desire to participate in this group became stronger and stronger. I finally got out our Methodist hymnal and began to read the prayers in the back. Taking a piece of paper and a pencil I began to compose a prayer using various phrases from the written prayers. Then I memorized the prayer I had written.

Tuesday evening Dorothy Jones invited me again to go with her to the young people's prayer fellowship. As the group prayed I waited nervously to express my formal, memorized prayer. I'm sure everyone wondered where I had learned such a prayer. But at the close of the meeting I felt as though I were on my way to knowing the same Christ that seemed to make such a difference in the lives of these young people.

It was not very long afterwards that they invited me to a revival meeting where I turned my life over to Christ. He did not make a spectacular, emotional entrance, but He made a very real one—one that touched the very center of my life. Prayer then became a natural expression of my relationship to Christ—as natural as conversation.

The prayer group, as well as another group which I joined—called a convert's class meeting—provided a growing experience for me and opened new discoveries in Christ. Inwardly, I developed a closer fellowship with Christ and learned the joy of living everyday in His presence. Outwardly, I became sensitive to the needs of others and felt a keen responsibility in leading them to Christ.

These small groups in which I was able to participate as a young Christian taught me that each member is always joined to the others in a genuine fellowship of concern expressed through prayer and mutual helpfulness. There is a desire to know and to do more fully the will of God.

Through the years I have enjoyed participating in various groups and have had the privilege of leading several kinds of groups.

This book has been prepared to help the reader discover the dynamics of a successful small-group fellowship. It is not a rigid rule book, but only a guide to help interested persons get started in this ministry of helping the many who are looking for a fulfilling Christian life. There are many kinds of "small groups" in the church that are being formed for a number of purposes. Many people are finding new meaning to life through these groups. In this book we will consider small groups in general, and more specifically prayer fellowships and the home Bible class.

—MARION K. RICH

Acknowledgments

I am grateful to Mrs. Paul Cunningham, who suggested the need for writing such material and encouraged me in the development of the manuscript.

My thanks to Mrs. Milton Parrish and Mrs. Frank Kish, who took time to read this manuscript and offered suggestions and encouragement. And also a thank-you to Mrs. Ron Ellis, who read the manuscript and was inspired by it to begin a new outreach group called a "Discovery Group" with young married couples.

I am deeply indebted to the many teachers and writers who have stimulated me through my years of study and participation in small groups; and to my husband, Harry, who is always a source of inspiration as I endeavor to do something for Christ.

—M. K. R.

PART I

DISCOVERY
in the
SMALL GROUP

◆   ◆   ◆

1

Why Have a Small Group?

The telephone rang. It startled me. I was deep in thought on the subject of small groups. The voice said, "A group of us are going to get together next week for a time of fellowship. Would you care to join us?"

That's interesting, I thought. Here I am writing about small groups and someone calls up about a group getting together.

"I haven't had a chance to really get to know some of the ladies," Shirley continued. "It would be nice if we could have lunch once a month—just for fellowship."

Fellowship—that's it, I thought. Fellowship is the basic need and urge for being together. This is what forms the foundation of the Christian community.

Shirley was new in our church. It was the warmth and friendliness of our people that attracted her to our congregation. She had gotten acquainted with many, but now she was feeling a need for a deeper level of fellowship. It would be impossible for her to know everyone in the church in an intimate way, but it is possible for her to know a few and even several with whom there is genuine love and communion. It is important that she find the love and care and mutuality and support that bind us together in Christ Jesus.

There is a difference between Christian fellowship and the fellowship of Christians. Many times we get together for Christian fellowship, just to do the things we enjoy, which may be all well and good. We eat, we have parties, play games, discuss all kinds of subjects—talk about church, the weather, world affairs, childhood days, our children, even talk about other people. We laugh, we have a good time, but how often we go home feeling somewhat empty or feel we've wasted time, and sometimes even feel guilty. Our fellowship together hasn't really been deepened and we haven't felt a oneness in Christ.

The early Christians were often together around the teachings of Christ—the Word, prayer, the sacraments. They were together to share their common life in Jesus. Somehow we need to rediscover the life the early Christians shared together—the kind of fellowship that gets deeper than football scores and the latest fashions.

I am sure there are many coming into our churches who feel a need for the fellowship of Christians—not the

14

superficial friendliness that often passes for fellowship, but the deeper relationship that develops between Christians as they sense that somehow they are together in a growing relationship with Christ.

We need one another. God planned it this way. He created us to need each other as well as Him. In the Body of Christ He has made us brothers and sisters, and He has given us spiritual gifts to use in ministering to each other.

We have heard two Greek words used a great deal in recent years—*koinonia* and *agape*. "Koinonia" is the New Testament word for fellowship. It communicates the deepest kind of togetherness. It has been described as "a deeply interdependent life together in which people share deeply, bear one another's burdens, and in which there is a real community." "Agape" is the word for divine love—God's love for us, or our love for Him, or our love for our fellow beings inspired by Him. Both *agape* love and *koinonia* involve genuine caring.

In our busyness and highly institutionalized programs we have largely lost the true New Testament fellowship. We often meet persons in our church services and even sit beside them and greet them, but fail to be concerned with or even discover the burdens they bear or the struggles in which they are engaged. It has been said that "loneliness in a crowd plagues not only the man on the street but also the man in the pew." There are broken persons inside the church, as well as outside. But we hide behind a facade and we share very little of our true inner selves with anyone. Is it because we do not have the opportunity?

In a small group where there is honest interaction and sharing with others, one may begin to reveal himself, and as he does he discovers an unknown freedom and release. One begins to experience genuine love and communion. God revealed himself to us that we might know Him. As we reveal ourselves to others we are known and loved by them. Honesty and openness are closely related to genuine fellowship and ultimately to evangelism.

I have heard people testify in a small group that they have hidden for years behind a facade and constantly sought to project a certain image. But after sharing and being honest in the group they stopped hiding and running from others. The fear of being discovered was replaced by freedom. They no longer remained in the isolation of their pretense. They exchanged deceit for truth.

The New Testament teaches and the Early Church practiced, "Love one another"; "Bear ye one another's burdens"; "Confess your faults one to another, and pray one for another, that ye may be healed." Such sharing and openness are not practical or even possible in meetings when the entire congregation meets together. In a small group such as the home Bible class or a prayer fellowship, one has the opportunity for spontaneous sharing and discovering what God is or is not doing in the lives of those present. Persons and personal relationships become our primary business rather than the promotion of a busy program.

In a small group one discovers depth, love, acceptance, freedom, and power. Then one begins to sense a responsibility to lead others into a group experience. Groups multiply and this provides outreach.

When a Christian has the experience of being in a small, dynamic, trusting group, he receives support and constructive help from others who love him in Christ. This kind of group is *koinonia,* or a fellowship where *agape* love is the prevailing atmosphere.

The Early Church had a certain vitality and spirit which seems to have been lost as the Church has grown in size and organization. We have lost the strong sense of community and commitment which characterized early

Christianity. The impersonalization and depersonalization of our society has made us become independent, individualistic, and even isolated. This has struck deep into the life of the Church and robbed us of our warmth and fellowship.

The Early Church began as a fellowship of believers who met together in one another's homes. In his epistles, Paul has frequent references to churches that met in homes (Rom. 16:5; 1 Cor. 16:19; Col. 4:15; Philem. 2). In the Book of Acts it is pointed out that Paul had preached the gospel faithfully "from house to house" (20:20). And in the last two years of his life, as a prisoner in his own house, he "received all that came in unto him, preaching . . . and teaching those things which concern the Lord Jesus Christ" (Acts 28:23, 30-31).

In recent years small groups have been meeting all across the nation trying to recapture the fresh, spiritual glow of apostolic times. We hear of men and women and young people meeting in shops and factories, schools, restaurants, and homes, in groups of 10 to 12, praying together, studying the Bible, and sharing their faith in Christ. Many are finding answers to their special needs through the fellowship of others in small, redemptive groups.

It is true that many of these groups lack trained leadership, but the very fact they are meeting indicates a desire for fellowship, or a desire to find direction and support in a confused world. What an opportunity for Christian laymen to study to show themselves approved unto God, and be used of Him to lead in small groups! Think what would take place in the lives of the members of your church if they would begin to bring others into a fresh relationship with God and with others. The outreach would be startling. There are people everywhere who are hungry for a meaningful faith.

Elton Trueblood, in *The Alternative to Futility*, states that the hope of our world lies in small, redemptive fellowships of laymen who will establish beachheads for Christ in our secular and pagan civilization.

Norman Vincent Peale feels that small groups of committed people constitute the hope of the church today. He says that people are seeking new insights from the Scriptures and are earnestly endeavoring to know and follow God's will. By the sharing of spiritual experience, individuals grow into mature Christians who can lead others out of the confusion of the times in which we live.

In a small group we come to know each other. We experience our identity both as human beings and as persons in whom Christ is living. We see each other in our inadequacies, but we also see Christ at work in us. We share our problems, our insecurities, our failures, but we go on to share our victories and tell what Christ is doing in our lives. He provides the dynamic for the group. With this kind of relationship with other Christians, our fellowship with Christ also grows.

Though fellowship between Christians is one of the greatest gifts that Christ gives to us in a small-group relationship, the group does not exist just for this fellowship. As we receive strength, healing, teaching, we also discover God's will for us in the world. The group is a base for support—then we are launched for our ministries in the world. Thus the small group exists for the world, even as the larger church does.

2

How Is the Small Group
Being Used Today?

The small group may be defined as three or more persons interacting in an informal, face-to-face relationship. They are more organized than a casual or informal meeting of several people who come together for some purpose of activity that is not expected to be continuous. For example, several neighbors may gather together in a neighbor's yard, decide to play a game, then spend the evening talking and laughing. The women may discuss children or fashions and the men may discuss sports or world affairs.[1]

In contrast to such a collection of people, consider a neighborhood Bible study group made up of a half dozen men and women who meet regularly to study the Bible.

Both may be described as groups containing individuals where there is interaction and they influence one another. However, the Bible study group is conscious of being an organized group. The membership is relatively stable and there is a specific group of interested people. They

---

1. Raymond McLaughlin, *Communication for the Church* (Grand Rapids: Zondervan Publishing House, 1968), pp. 151-52.

have a common purpose and a set of goals. There is a high degree of successful communication between all the members. The neighborhood gathering does not think of itself as an organized group. It has no sense of belonging, those who participate may change from time to time, or it may break up altogether. It has no specific purpose or goals, little awareness of interdependence, and its communication process may not include all members of the gathering.[2]

In researching the value of small groups we find that the small group is the major source of the values and attitudes that people have. We know that the roles which children learn within the family and the play group influence the roles which they take into other surroundings and circumstances. Thus the small group serves as an important mediating function between the individual and the larger society.[3]

The small group is being used today in many areas of life for a variety of purposes. In the field of education, the small class is found to be effective and vital. Training in human relations for supervisors, managers, and leaders focus on sensitivity-training groups. Social workers insist that when treatment is directed at the family or the gang there is hope in regulating and restraining delinquency. Shepherd points out that various organizations are using committees to do much of their work.

For a number of years the study of small groups has been one of the major areas of current research in the field of sociology and social psychology. Psychiatrists and clinical psychologists find group therapy to have many important advantages in private counseling. O. Hobart Mowrer,

---

2. *Ibid.*, pp. 152-53.
3. Clovis R. Shepherd, *Small Groups, Some Sociological Perspectives* (Scranton, Pa.: Chandler Publishing Co., 1964), p. 1.

psychologist, says that the crucial element in "mental health" is the degree of "openness" and "communion" which a person has with his fellowman. He feels that the "new" group therapy is here to stay—that without it our very survival may be in jeopardy.[4]

The small group such as the prayer fellowship or the home Bible class possesses all the ingredients necessary for group therapy. As we approach the Bible together we find that God uses the Word to bring our life and thoughts and actions into harmony with Him and with one another. There is the healing of guilt as one understands what the New Testament means by confession and as one is honest with God in the presence of several others. Being honest with another about himself can remove the blocks and bring freedom and release.

Most people crave group fellowship. They like the feeling of being accepted and belonging to a group. There is an inner longing in the hearts of many Christians to share deep and intimate relationships with Christ. Christians are desiring dialogue, not monologue. These opportunities are found in a small group.

The word *dialogue* has taken on new meaning in group therapy today. The word is being redefined and applied in many areas of life. Dialogue refers to communication between persons that produces a meeting of meanings. Reuel Howe, in his book *The Miracle of Dialogue,* tells about a group of ministers that were told that until the Church becomes a community, it will not be able to communicate adequately. He said, "Left unanswered was the question: How does the Church or any other group of people become a community? And the answer is simple: it becomes a

---

4. *The New Group Therapy* (New York: Van Nostrand Reinhold Co., 1964), pp. 3, 6.

community when as persons the members enter into dialogue with one another and assume responsibility for their common life. . . . It is through dialogue that man accomplishes the miracle of personhood and community.[5]

I heard a young mother recently testify in a small group. She said, "There's something wonderful about the closeness we feel to one another in our group. I can just be myself and express my deep needs to all of you without feeling that I will be condemned or criticized. There is a deep level of understanding—a feeling that someone really cares about my hurts, my weaknesses, my failures. I am beginning to let God's Word straighten out the mess I've made of my life. I only wish I had found Christ sooner."

Many people do not have an opportunity to communicate with others beyond "cliche conversation." We talk in cliches such as: "How are you?" . . . "It's good to see you!" . . . "How is your family?" . . . "What a pretty dress." Usually the other person senses the conventionality of our greetings and simply gives the standard answers. There is no sharing of persons at all. One remains safely in the shelter of his sophistication.

In a small group where people discover the real meaning of dialogue, they become completely open and honest with each other. As the Holy Spirit works through the Word they seek to be identified with Jesus in every part of their daily living.

Communication on a deep level in a small group brings about real and genuine relationships. Not only is there mutual communication of persons and the sharing and experiencing of personhood, but a growth in one's self-identity results. We understand ourselves better as we are willing to communicate ourselves to another.

When people get to know each other in the personal

5. (New York: The Seabury Press, 1963), p. 5.

informality of small groups they begin to watch out for each other. They step in to help when material needs occur; they pray for each other and bear one another's burdens; they visit each other when sickness or problems come; they laugh or weep with one another.

A few weeks ago one of the ladies of a small group took seriously ill. Two of the nurses in the group took her under their personal care. They got her into a hospital, had the pastor visit her, and carried a real concern for her in every way. The lady was having serious marital problems in addition to her illness. The group cared, prayed, and did what they could to help the situation. When I visited her in the hospital she said to me, "I never had such friends like this before in my life—I am overwhelmed by their love and concern." She went home from the hospital well, happy, and even reconciled with her husband.

Dr. Paul Tournier, Swiss psychiatrist, says: "How beautiful, how grand and liberating this experience is, when people learn to help each other. It is impossible to overemphasize the immense need humans have to be really listened to, to be taken seriously, to be understood."[6]

The small group in the church should never be thought of as a gathering that replaces the church. The small group is a spiritual organism within the larger body of the church. Bible study in small groups should never be a substitute for either the congregational life of the church or the individual devotional life of each member. However, in Christian circles, the small group is an effective medium for communication, fellowship, expression of love, growth in grace, a fresh encounter with the Holy Spirit through the Word, evangelism, and service.

6. Quoted by S. J. Powell, *Why Am I Afraid to Tell You Who I Am?* (Niles, Ill.: Argus Communications, 1969), p. 5.

A living group is never stagnant. It is ever growing and reaching out to touch more and more lives. But most important, it is in touch with the One who said, "I am the way, the truth, and the life" (John 14:6).

3

What Kinds of Groups
in the Church?

Elton Trueblood says: "Somewhere in the world there should be a society consciously and deliberately devoted to the task of seeing how love can be made real and demonstrating love in practice." He feels that the most important thing to God is "the creation of centers of loving fellowship, which in turn infect the world."[7]

The Christian life is a corporate experience. One personality touches one, another, another, and all of us together, with different gifts and functions make up the whole church. However, we often need other people to draw us out, to encourage us to open our mouths or to take responsibilities. The formal church needs to be supplemented by these small, informal groups where we build each other up and help each other move toward God's goal of Christlikeness.

Two broad goals of group life are important to the church—one is fellowship and the other is service. Fellow-

---

7. *The Company of the Committed* (New York: Harper and Row, Publishers, 1961), p. 113.

ship, even on a high level, is not enough to keep a group intact. There must be goals to attain, objectives to pursue, and services to perform. I am refering to the small groups that are formed for the purpose of encouraging the growth of the members; not committees with decisions to make or tasks to perform.

Growth groups use various means to achieve their objective of improving the lives of their members. Some groups use *Bible study* as the primary means—meeting to learn more about what the Bible says. There are also *home Bible classes* that meet with an evangelistic purpose. There are *personal groups*—groups that form to get to know each other in depth. There are *therapy groups* where people share in confidence their problems, or confess their faults to one another. There are *action groups*—groups assembled to work on a particular task; or the "Action Groups" which Campus Crusade for Christ has developed with a strategy for building Christian disciples.

There are *study groups* or *discussion groups* that meet to talk about Christian books they are reading or to discuss pertinent subjects related to the Christian life. There are *prayer groups* that meet primarily to pray for the needs of the church, personal problems, or world needs. Some groups are completely *unstructured* with no definite leader, no study book, and no set program—just people talking with each other about what is important to them. Other groups use periods of *silence* to listen to what God may be trying to say to each of the members. Many groups combine several of these methods during each meeting.

Various names have been given to small groups such as: "Growth Cells," "Living Circles," "Share Fellowship," "Yokefellows," "T.O.G." (Talk it Over Group), "Circle of Concern," "Interaction Group," "Encounter Group," "Koinonia," "Serendipity Labs," "Upper Room," "The Little Churches," "Class Meetings," "Convert's Class

Meeting," "CHUM Group" (Christian Home Unit Meetings), "Home Bible Class," "Prayer Fellowship," "Becomers," "Disciples," "Links of Love," etc.

"No one has a copyright on the small-group movement!" says Elton Trueblood. "All are experimenting together and all are learning. But when we learn, even in a small way, we dare not keep what we have discovered to ourselves."[8]

---

8. D. Elton Trueblood, Introduction to *Groups That Work,* compiled by Walden Howard (Grand Rapids: Zondervan Publishing House, 1967), p. 7.

4

How to Get Started and Lead

One group I know started over a cup of coffee. Bethel is a quiet, unobtrusive young mother of four small children. She lives in an apartment complex and carries a burden for souls. One day her neighbor, Pam, was having coffee with Bethel. The subject turned to spiritual things and Bethel shared her faith with Pam. Some months later in a home Bible class, Pam told me, "I first became aware of my need of Christ and opened my heart to Him over a cup of coffee at Bethel's kitchen table."

Pam had said to Bethel, "There are others in our neighborhood who need to know Christ and I myself am so ignorant of the Bible, we ought to have a Bible study group!"

Bethel was delighted. She had worked as a nurse in the nearby hospital and was acquainted with other nurses and medical assistants who also lived in the apartment complex. Several she knew worked afternoon and evening shifts and might be able to come one morning a week to study the Bible. She invited them and they came. She asked me to teach the class or at least to get it started. It was an exciting experience and an evangelistic opportunity. I taught the class for one year, then Bethel took over.

The group has been meeting now for three years. A deep fellowship has developed in the group—a caring for one another, a bearing of one another's burdens. When one is sick—they all hurt. If one is bereaved—they all sorrow. If one is in trouble—they all try to help. There is the kind of love that Jesus said would characterize His disciples.

What does it take to get a group started? It takes an openness with at least one or two others. It takes faith and initiative; it takes personal conviction and concern. It takes a willingness to experiment. Oftentimes people express a desire to get together in a group for fellowship or indicate a desire to study God's Word—seize this as an opportunity to get a group started. Don't be afraid to start small.

Jesus himself gave us a pattern for a small group. His closest friends—Peter, James, and John—were central in His work. Jesus associated with man—healing, teaching, reaching out to the multitudes—but He lived in close fellowship with His disciples. He shared His real life with them. He told them about His struggles, His temptations, His dilemmas. In the last weeks of Jesus' life, rather than preaching to the multitudes, He spent much time with His disciples. He told them about the Holy Spirit and what He would do in their lives. These men were to become like fire throughout the Roman Empire.

In a very real sense Christ would call many of us into the role of training—then leading others, that as Christians we may share the life of Christ with the world. In God's kingdom, there is the drawing power of the Holy Spirit. It is He who gives gifts to men and women—gifts of teaching and encouraging and leading others with enthusiasm, with love, and with faith.

Many books today on the subject of small groups recommend groups without leaders or the rotation of leadership. Perhaps some groups do develop spontaneously but many such groups struggle along and finally break down unless someone takes the initiative to keep the group on target in regard to its purpose and goals. Someone needs to set the pace in openness, in sharing, in honesty, and in dedication to Christ and to one another. Someone needs to allow God's love to flow through to others in real interest and concern. Someone needs to plan how to break through the ever-present reserve.

Of course, rotating the leadership on a mechanical basis guarantees little. The whole subject of leadership and its importance is in line with God's truth in both the Old and New Testaments. Many need to discover their calling and allow the Holy Spirit to utilize the gifts and talents that are within them.

In the small group the leader should avoid dominating the group or establishing himself as the authority on all matters that come before the group. The leader ought to be a full participant and share his own concerns and needs with the group. The leader's task includes the responsibility to help develop honest, authentic fellowship in the group. He must create a climate in which group members feel free to minister to each other. The leader should help each one to assume an increasing share of responsibility and leadership, and to grow away from dependence upon him.

God wants to equip ordinary men and women and help them lead others in areas of Christian living. Most often every leader of a group begins with great fear and this could very well be its strength. The greater the sense of weakness, the more reliance there is on God. Trust the Holy Spirit to empower and use you.

The following are general suggestions for starting a new group and leading the meetings. (Specific suggestions for starting a Prayer Fellowship or Home Bible Class are given in Parts 2 and 3.)

1. Decide what kind of group would be helpful to you or is needed among your friends.

2. If you've had an experience of God's grace and are convinced that a small group can make an impact on your life and on your friends, experiment in inviting a few friends to your home for a time of fellowship together.

3. Talk to your pastor about your interest in starting a group. He can help you find materials to use and suggest the best time for the group to meet.

4. Set a definite time to meet. Continuity and interest are best if the group meets each week. One hour is usually adequate.

5. Set a definite length of time such as 6 weeks or 12 weeks. People respond better to groups set for a certain period of time. Most people will want the group to continue for a longer time if the meetings are successful.

6. Encourage members to invite their friends. However, the group should be kept small enough so that all may participate and really come to know each other significantly. Seven to 10 people is a good size.

7. A home is probably the best place to meet because of the informal atmosphere which helps people to participate.

8. Begin and close meetings on time.

9. Create a climate of acceptance and an atmosphere that is warm, friendly and relaxed. Serve coffee or simple refreshments.

10. Encourage shy members to participate, but do not embarrass or put pressure on anyone. Sometimes it takes several meetings before some individuals feel free enough to open up.

11. Encourage expression of real feelings and listen attentively. Be honest about yourself.

12. Keep discussion on target. Always focus on spiritual growth.

13. Avoid controversial matters. Never allow debate or argument.

14. Never allow the group to reflect the idea that "we are more spiritual."

15. Have a good time in the fellowship. Make the most of other opportunities to be a friend to the members of the group.

16. Keep the group Christ-centered. It is He who can meet our needs and change our lives. Our aim is to know Him better and allow Him to live through us.

17. Pray much for the Holy Spirit to work in the group. He will open hearts to love and be loved. He will weld hearts together. He will quicken understanding of God's Word and help us to respond to the Lord.

The techniques of "group dynamics" can be helpful to use, but unless each member comes to a fresh commitment to God and applies God's Word to his daily life, the group fails. There must be a desire to communicate the message of the gospel to others. Even the group in which people are finding Christ as their Savior will fall short of the mark unless the group forms an organic part of the Body of Christ and becomes an arm of the Church. Groups by themselves are never an end in themselves.

Small groups are a means of putting real individuals in touch with other real individuals, and of transforming the church from merely an efficient organization into a loving, dynamic fellowship where men and women become vitally alive with faith, hope, and love. Those who find a deep mutual trust and sharing in a small-group experience rate it as one of the most precious of their possessions. It is this close-knit fellowship of caring that made the Early Church so appealing and so powerful. This has been the mark of the vital Church all through history.

PART II

DISCOVERY
in the
PRAYER FELLOWSHIP
GROUP

◆　◆　◆

5

Why Have a Prayer Fellowship?

There was a challenging sparkle in her eyes as she spoke. "I've heard a lot about the prayer fellowship group in this church," she said. "I'd like to attend, but please don't call on me to pray aloud." I assured her that no one would call on her and she could just relax and enjoy the fellowship with others in the group. However, after several weeks of being in the group she overcame her reticence and began to participate in the prayer time. Today, to hear her pray, no one would ever suspect that she was ever reluctant to pray audibly.

There is power in effectual, united prayer! Churches that are moving forward spiritually have a strong prayer backing from people who believe in God's power to work and to change lives.

It is important that Christians pray together. Praying together produces love. Praying together generates faith. As we pray together we sense a genuine "togetherness," self-consciousness drops away, and we begin to trust others and pray about our deep needs. Whenever Christians pray together there is an enlarged outreach and a desire to share God's love and kindness in practical ways. Praying together results in purposeful living.

A prayer group often answers a real need as a discipline of the spiritual life. One lady testified in our prayer group: "I have lived an 'up and down' Christian experience for years—and I must admit I was mostly down. The turning point in my life came when I decided to attend this prayer group regularly and discipline myself to be here each week. Attending these meetings led to keeping a quiet time every day—reading my Bible and praying for others. I've begun to love the Bible and, for the first time in my life, to understand it. Gradually God has been untangling my life with its resentments and fears and insecurities. I now have deep peace and an assurance of God's forgiveness for my past sins."

There is nothing new about a prayer group. It is a principle based upon God's Word. Jesus introduced the idea to His disciples. He taught His disciples: "If two of you shall agree on earth as touching any thing that they shall ask, it shall be done for them of my Father which is in heaven. For where two or three are gathered together in my name, there am I in the midst of them" (Matt. 18:19-20).

Jesus had times of prayer with His disciples—especially Peter, James, and John. In Luke 9:28, it says: "He took Peter and John and James, and went up into a mountain to pray." We read in Matt. 26:36-38 the account where Jesus took the three disciples with Him to the Garden of Gethsemane to watch and *pray*. In His own ministry Jesus demonstrated this principle of praying together. In His "High Priestly Prayer" (John 17), He lifted up His small group of disciples when talking to His Heavenly Father.

St. Paul knew the power of the discipline of prayer in his own life. In Rom. 15:30 he said, "I beseech you, brethren, . . . that ye strive together with me in your prayers to God for me." The missionary party which traveled with Paul formed a prayer group to pray daily for the concerns of the church (Col. 1:9; 1 Thess. 1:2; 2 Thess. 1:11). The apostle James told the church to "pray for one another" (5:16).

In the Book of Acts we see the Christians continually praying for each other and with one another. "They continued stedfastly in . . . fellowship . . . and in prayers" (Acts 2:42). In the 12th chapter of Acts we read about Peter's miraculous escape from prison because a group of believers were praying together for him.

In times of spiritual awakening throughout history, it has been prayer groups which have helped renew the fresh spiritual glow of apostolic times. We read of the great evangelical revival in the late 18th century which swept across the world and ultimately gave birth to the Methodist church. It all began with a little Holy Club in Oxford where the group was praying and waiting on God. The Wesleys were so convinced of the value of small groups that every Methodist society was organized into small bands and class meetings. During the time of Methodism's greatest spiritual and evangelistic vitality, for more than a century, small groups meeting for prayer and Bible study were the real life of each local church.

The great revival in America in 1857 and 1858 came as a result of small-group prayer meetings led by laymen. This national awakening affected every church in the land. Millions of souls were led to the Lord.

I had the privilege of being a missionary in Haiti for the Church of the Nazarene from 1957 to 1971. During the years between 1960 and 1969 our church experienced almost continuous revival. Many times we felt as though we were living in another chapter of the Book of Acts. The growth in the membership of our church during these years was tremendous, and Haiti became the largest mission field in the Church of the Nazarene. It was no secret that again prayer and a great emphasis on the Word were the major factors that precipitated revival.

A great spirit of prayer prevailed in all of our churches on the island. Early morning prayer bands would meet at the local church at 5:30 each day. Wednesday mornings were given to prayer and fasting from 5 a.m. to 12 noon. Some of the churches also prayed and fasted on Friday mornings. Our Bible school students asked to have a prayer and fasting service placed in their class schedule every Wednesday morning. Before every evangelistic thrust, every revival campaign or Sunday school rally, the people spent a night in prayer. There were literally thousands in attendance with hundreds of people being saved in these campaigns.

Some of the most precious moments I have experienced with God were during the years that I joined the early morning prayer band each day at 5:30 in our Bible school chapel. During this time I also sensed the greatest growth in my own spiritual life. There were times of earnest heart-searching, times of intercession and waiting on God, times of listening to Him speak, times of praise and thanksgiving for the miracles and mighty moving of His Spirit in the churches. Discipline became a delight. I will never forget the earnest prayers of some of the dedicated young men in our Bible school. Their depth of commitment to preach the gospel was heart-stirring.

Many people came from the villages round about our headquarters to pray early in the morning. One little old lady about 80 years old walked for miles down the steep mountain trail. We called her "Gran." She had recently been converted and the Christian life was new to her, but she learned to schedule prayer into the beginning of her day. I marvelled at her disciplined devotional life. With thousands of Haitian Christians rising early in the morning to pray together, it is no wonder that multitudes were brought under the sway of the marvelous gospel of Christ.

Prayer is the key to revival! If God's people would return to this proven method of united and effectual prayer, God would again send a great revival to our land. Revival can come without singing. It can come without preaching. But revival will never come without prayer! "If my people, which are called by my name, shall humble themselves, and pray, and seek my face, and turn from their wicked ways; then will I hear from heaven, and will forgive their sin, and will heal their land" (2 Chron. 7:14).

It is significant that many revivals throughout the history of the church have occurred because of small prayer groups. How wonderful it would be if God's Spirit would again visit our land through the simple means of prayer groups and home Bible classes. A prayer group will ultimately express itself in action and everyone will eventually benefit by the renewed life it imparts to the whole church.

6

Who For?

The purpose of a prayer fellowship is not directly evangelistic. But as witnessing takes place, some may desire from time to time to bring in their non-Christian friends who are seriously considering accepting Christ as their Savior. However, members of the group should not invite non-Christians indiscriminately or it will change the character of the group. The purpose of the prayer group is primarily to intercede for the needs of the group, the church, and the country; to build up believers so that evangelization will take place out in the world.

A prayer group is never designated "for members only." Other believers who want to come should be welcomed. It is not necessary for a prayer fellowship to be age-graded. Differences in age and experience are a help to the group.

It is especially important to invite new Christians into the prayer fellowship. They need a place where they can try out their new way of life and learn what it demands and involves. A prayer group is an ideal place where a new Christian can go and learn how to be a Christian and where he can learn to pray. In the prayer group he hears others pray for total surrender and a complete dedication. It is a place to grow spiritually, to realize where he falls short, and where he most needs help and power.

There are many hungry men and women—some who are even spiritually broken, who could greatly benefit from a prayer group that reaches out and invites them into the fellowship. The group would be an opportunity for them to recover their personal integrity and identity which they have all but lost through isolation.

Many churches are growing today and have an effective outreach ministry because consecrated laymen are the foundation of the church's growth and ministry. Their prayer groups are the most significant of the groups in the church.

In some churches there are prayer groups for couples that meet one evening a week in a home. Many youth groups have vital prayer cells. There are men's groups and ladies' groups that meet each week for a time of intercessory prayer. There are groups that meet for a time of prayer and fasting and pray particularly for the worldwide missionary program of the church.

As one participates in a prayer fellowship, something very real and significant takes place. One becomes keenly aware of the Spirit's presence in the midst of the group. There is a unanimity of expression—as Jesus said, "If two of you shall agree on earth . . ."—and there is a common purpose shared by all. The prayer group becomes a redemptive fellowship of love in which the living Christ is known.

7

How to Get Started

It was not very long after we moved to our present pastorate that a young woman came to me. She was weary, weighed down with problems, anxious, and insecure. There was a deep seriousness about her manner that day as we talked about her deep needs. Without finishing her conversation she burst out with—"I wish some of us could get together once in a while for a time of prayer. I just feel that I need some kind of a spiritual lift."

"Sounds great," I said. "Let's announce a ladies' prayer fellowship to meet at the parsonage on Tuesday mornings at 10 o'clock."

Five ladies came. It was a good start.

That was almost five years ago. We've since moved to the fellowship hall of our church because of size as well as facilities for baby-sitting service for young mothers. An average of 18 to 20 women attend each week in a beautiful spirit of love and unity, caring for one another, sharing what Christ is doing in their spiritual lives, carrying a burden for souls, and praying for the spiritual needs of the church. After coffee and devotions we break up into prayer cells of six to eight for our prayer time.

This prayer group is not an end in itself, but a channel through which the Holy Spirit can work. The group radiates with spiritual vitality. More than half of the ladies who come to pray are also involved in the outreach visitation program of our church later in the day. Their relationship with Christ has become a very positive thing in their lives. Their witness is natural, confident, and spontaneous. They have a sense of mission.

Because of this group, a new quality has come into the women's life of the church, with individuals becoming capable people willingly and eagerly assuming leadership in many areas of church work which before they were not at all adequate to handle.

Here are 10 suggestions on how to start a prayer group:

1. Make a surrender of yourself to God, including your total prayer life. Let God have His way with you.

2. Meditate upon the ways God has used effectual, united prayer and what He has been pleased to do with and through others in prayer groups. When you are convinced that God does use this means of prayer, then . . .

3. Ask God to help you get together with someone or some others who are interested in joining together for a time of prayer.

4. Talk to your pastor about your interest and desire to start a prayer group. He will know the best time to fit into the schedule of your church and give you suggestions to help your group.

5. Invite other Christians to join your prayer group.

6. Set a definite time and meet together regularly for prayer and the sharing of burdens and blessings. Weekly or biweekly meetings are suggested. You can meet at any place where there is reasonable privacy and at a time that

is most convenient to all the members. Each meeting should last about an hour.

7. Create a relaxed atmosphere of informality. A coffee time for the first 15 minutes helps people to get to know each other better. But remember your purpose is spiritual, not social. Do not let anyone defeat the spirit of the meeting with idle talk or gossiping. If sharing degenerates to gossiping, the group will destroy itself. As a leader, set a spiritual tone.

8. Keep an emphasis on God's Word. Let a short passage of scripture or prayer promise be the basis for your time of prayer. You may vary your procedure with a brief meditation or devotional, or time of sharing that is based on some truth from God's Word.

9. Seek to grow in the knowledge of God and find some way to express the purpose of the group in Christian service or personal evangelism.

10. Keep in mind that there is no limit to what God can do through your prayer group if you will give it your best. Let the Holy Spirit unite and empower the group through the Word.

8

How to Keep Going

I have talked with a number of people who have experienced positive and exciting things in their groups. They felt that the Holy Spirit gave their groups a certain vitality. Lives of men and women involved were significantly changed, and the group had a sense of mission. There have been other people who joined small groups with great hope and expectation but were keenly disappointed because they had not found what they were hoping for.

It cannot be emphasized enough that without prayer and the moving of the Spirit, there will be nothing of permanence happening in the group. Rosalind Rinker, in her book *Praying Together,* says: "Without a sense of mission there will be stagnation and boredom. An ingrown group of Christians is a dead group . . . and boredom will quickly provide an exit for those who are still alive."[9]

A good leader is a key to a successful prayer fellowship. What you are and what you do will ultimately deter-

---

9. (Grand Rapids: Zondervan Publishing House, 1968), p. 90.

mine the effectiveness of the group. Your attitude and spirit will be contagious. When you have the real thing those around you will likely catch what you have. You must point the way for others to follow by your own obedient walk with God. As members of the group gain confidence, pass the leadership to others from time to time to bring a short devotional, and if your group becomes large, break up into prayer cells and appoint others to lead.

Cultivate a feeling of solidarity among the members of your group. Do things to show your love for one another. There are many ways to do it. Just the remembrance of birthdays, anniversaries, and other special days is appreciated. Our ladies' prayer group has drawn names for "secret prayer pals," and we remember that person on special days through the year as well as praying especially for that person each day. Then at Christmastime we reveal ourselves to one another and draw new names for the following year. Thoughtfulness in little things will bind you closer together in bigger things. Small groups of four or five get together once a month for lunch either at a restaurant or at a home after the prayer meeting for the purpose of fellowship and to get better acquainted.

In your daily devotions, remember the prayer requests made by members of your group. Prayer lists are helpful as a reminder of these needs. Trust the prayer group with the intimate yearnings of your heart. Let them share your work and your calling. Tell them about your doubts and burdens, as well as your dreams and aspirations. Protect and preserve the honesty and mutual confidence of the persons in your prayer group. Never carry in conversation beyond the border of your group that which is shared in confidence.

Lift up for your friends the highest possibilities of Christian experience which you have known. There will be times when someone will ask a question about the Bible or raise a question about some point of doctrine. If you cannot answer the question scripturally, be honest and tell them that you do not know, but that you will try to find the answer by next week. Make an effort to do so. Perhaps someone else in the group may know the answer. Keep a responsiveness and an openness in the group.

A prayer fellowship is an instrument of tremendous power and blessing only when each member is laboring for the good of the others. A genuine love and mutual commitment to each other will be seen in the way they relate to each other between meetings.

Our group has a prayer chain set up in order to alert one another in time of crisis. How many times the telephones have rung with urgent requests: "My daughter is in critical condition in the hospital, please pray for her." "My little niece was abducted on her way home from school today—pray that we find her."

Olive is a young grandmother who attends our prayer fellowship. She was backing a camper out of her driveway one day when her little three-year-old grandson excitedly ran out behind her and was struck down by the truck. In panic, she picked up the little lad and as her son drove the vehicle to the hospital he flagged down a policeman who escorted them. Little Johnny was taken into emergency and as soon as Olive could get to a telephone she called for the prayer chain to pray.

Across the city earnest prayers went up to God in behalf of Johnny. When I arrived at the hospital Olive was in great distress. She looked like she had aged 10 years in those agonizing moments. With tears streaming down her face she said to me, "I know those wheels went over Johnny. I felt them! He even has the tire marks on his back." Johnny was x-rayed thoroughly. How we rejoiced when we learned there were no broken bones. He was badly bruised but in two days he left the hospital with no serious problems.

A miracle—yes, we believe it was. There have been hundreds of them, big ones and little ones. We do not forget to give thanks during the prayer time in our group for the answers which have taken place during the week. Thanksgiving feeds our faith. The Psalmist says: "O give thanks unto the Lord; call upon his name: make known his deeds among the people" (Ps. 105:1).

The most effective group size for a prayer fellowship is 7 to 12 people. A group may start with as few as three. When the group grows to 12 active members, it should pray about starting a second group. A new group can be formed by simply dividing the present group in two. This can be done on the basis of geography. One of the best suggestions is to look upon the new group as an "outreach" not as a "division." If the group is meeting in the fellowship hall of the church, the group may be divided into prayer cells after the coffee time and disperse into different rooms for their time of prayer.

To keep the prayer group going with a freshness and vitality takes the power of the Holy Spirit. As you orient your life and witness around the Word of God and seek to express your devotion to Christ, superficiality and irrelevance will be avoided. You may need to change your procedure and methods from time to time to meet the need of the group. There is nothing absolute about any particular pattern.

We must always seek more of God, more love, more truth, and more ways of experiencing and expressing Christ through our lives. Methods are important only as they help us to attain this objective. Remember always that the blessings come through prayer. Merely going through a routine will not suffice. The effectivenss of what we do depends on how we pray.

46

9

How to Ask and Receive

Prayer is simply communion with God. It is communication with Him. It is the opening of our hearts and minds to Him and making Him the Center of our attention.

I have heard many say, "Please, never call on me to pray in public. I get too scared and I can't think of what to say," or "Don't call on me because I just can't make my words sound right when I pray aloud." These same people have come into our prayer fellowship and have begun to participate in prayer. They have learned that prayer is not merely a matter of words but, as Rosalind Rinker suggests, "Prayer is the natural language of the heart."

In a prayer group we get to know each other on a deeper level of fellowship and we get to know God better. Shyness soon drops away. Prayer should never be regarded as making a speech before God, nor using beautiful, eloquent words to influence the minds of those who are present. Prayer should be offered to God and to Him alone. When a group comes together to pray, the marvelous power of individual prayer is intensified. There is a peculiar power in corporate prayer.

God has promised to answer our prayers, but we do need to follow His directions when we pray. The Word of God is our chief help in cultivating our faith and in seeking to know the mind and will of God.

How do we ask in order that we might receive? Here are some things the Scriptures tell us we must do.

1. *Believe that God does answer prayer.* We come to Him in faith—faith in His promises.

"If thou canst believe, all things are possible to him that believeth" (Mark 9:23).

"If ye have faith, and doubt not . . . it shall be done. And all things whatsoever ye shall ask in prayer, believing, ye shall receive" (Matt. 21:21-22).

"What things soever ye desire, when ye pray, believe that ye receive them, and ye shall have them" (Mark 11:24).

"Let him ask in faith, nothing wavering" (Jas. 1:6).

2. *Depend only upon the merit and mediation of Christ.* We pray in His name.

"It is Christ that died, yea rather, that is risen again, who is even at the right hand of God, who also maketh intercession for us" (Rom. 8:34).

"Whatsoever ye shall ask in my name, that will I do, that the Father may be glorified in the Son. If ye shall ask anything in my name, I will do it" (John 14:13-14).

"If ye abide in me, and my words abide in you, ye shall ask what ye will, and it shall be done unto you" (John 15:7).

3. *Allow the Holy Spirit to search your heart and assure you that your heart is clean.* Obey all the truth you understand.

"If I regard iniquity in my heart, the Lord will not hear me" (Ps. 66:18).

"The effectual fervent prayer of a righteous man availeth much" (Jas. 5:16).

"The eyes of the Lord are upon the righteous, and his ears are open unto their cry" (Ps. 34:15).

"We know that God heareth not sinners: but if any man be a worshipper of God, and doeth his will, him he heareth" (John 9:31).

"Beloved, if our heart condemn us not, then have we confidence toward God. And whatsoever we ask, we receive of him, because we keep his commandments, and do those things that are pleasing in his sight" (1 John 3:21-22).

4. *Seek to know the will of God.* God reveals His will to us through the Holy Spirit and through His Word.

"This is the confidence that we have in him, that, if we ask any thing according to his will, he heareth us: and if we know that he hear us, whatsoever we ask, we know that we have the petitions that we desired of him" (1 John 5:14-15).

"Likewise the Spirit also helpeth our infirmities: for we know not what we should pray for as we ought: but the Spirit itself maketh intercession for us with groanings which cannot be uttered. And he that searcheth the hearts knoweth what is the mind of the Spirit, because he maketh intercession for the saints according to the will of God" (Rom. 8:26-27).

5. *Earnestness, boldness, fervency, and importunity are chief ingredients in prayer.* The Word of God implies that prayer is an ardent and vigorous exercise of the soul. Never give up! Expect an answer!

"Ask, and it shall be given unto you; seek, and ye shall find; knock, and it shall be opened unto you" (Matt. 7:7).

"Men ought always to pray, and not to faint. . . . And shall not God avenge his own elect, which cry day and night unto him, though he bear long with them?" (Luke 18:1, 7).

"Let us therefore come boldly unto the throne of grace, that we may obtain mercy, and find grace to help in time of need" (Heb. 4:16).

"The effectual fervent prayer of a righteous man availeth much" (Jas. 5:16).

"As soon as Zion travailed, she brought forth her children" (Isa. 66:8).

6. *Praise God and thank Him for everything of good report.*

"Be careful for nothing; but in every thing by prayer and supplication with thanksgiving let your requests be made known unto God. And the peace of God, which passeth all understanding, shall keep your hearts and minds through Christ Jesus" (Phil. 4:6-7).

There are no formal or rigid rules for conducting a prayer group. However, the leader should be sensitive and aware of the moving of the Holy Spirit in the group. The group comes together primarily to pray and to be conscious that we are in the presence of God.

In the prayer fellowship, vary the procedure during the prayer time—according to the amount of time you have for prayer, the number in the group, and the individuals present. Respect the reticence of the beginner by making it a rule never to begin a prayer period with a remark which implies that every person should pray aloud.

If there are new Christians who are unaccustomed to praying audibly, explain "conversational prayer."* Con-

---

*Suggested book: *Prayer: Conversing with God* by Rosalind Rinker, published by Zondervan Publishing House, 1959.

versational prayer is different from the traditional "prayer meeting prayer" in that it is approached as a conversation with God, not an address to Him. It involves using sentence prayers covering one subject at a time. It is just talking to God as though He were sitting right there with us in conversation. Prayer requests are brought up as we pray. A participant may pray more than once just as in conversation you probably would speak more than once. There are fewer cliches—more honesty and simplicity. With this approach to prayer, new Christians will begin praying aloud in the group more quickly than if they feel they must pray for a longer period of time.

In varying the prayer period, open the meeting for spontaneous prayer as the Spirit will lead different ones to lead out in prayer. Sometimes call on specific persons to lead in prayer.

A leader should guide the group in instruction with love and tactfulness from time to time. Sometimes one or more persons insist on long prayers, or one person prays too often in conversational prayer and dominates the group, or perhaps the stating of prayer requests to the group becomes a time-consuming practice. The important thing is that the Holy Spirit be in full charge. He will give real freedom to pray honestly and sincerely. Tensions will be released and a holy love will go from heart to heart as we "sit together in heavenly places in Christ Jesus" (Eph. 2:6).

PART III

DISCOVERY
in the
HOME BIBLE CLASS

◆   ◆   ◆

10

Why Have a Home Bible Class?

"Looks like this will be my mission field for this year," I remarked to my husband as we drove into the mobile-home park in Belton, Mo., a suburb of Kansas City.

As missionaries we had been given permission to live in Kansas City during a year's furlough while my husband studied in the missions department at Nazarene Theological Seminary.

We made friends with the neighbors as the days went by. One day I had an opportunity to witness to a lady in the laundromat. She seemed hungry for spiritual life and invited me to visit her someday. The Lord laid a burden on my heart for her and I felt I must again share Christ with her. After much prayer, one afternoon I called on her. She talked and talked and I despaired of ever getting through to her.

When I stood to leave the conversation turned to spiritual things and soon she was in tears. I explained the way of salvation and pointed to the scriptures from my New Testament. Tears began to stream down her face. That afternoon Marie prayed and found Christ as her Savior. With a glow on her face she exclaimed, "This is wonderful! If I get my friends to come, would you be willing to teach a Bible study class to us?"

What an opportunity to share Christ! A course on the Gospel of John was started and grew until 10 ladies were studying one afternoon a week. Most of them had not attended church for years. The Holy Spirit began to illuminate the Word to their hearts. They began talking honestly with deep involvement about their discouragements, their loneliness, their most pressing problems, their spiritual needs. They found that Christianity was not what they had thought it was at all, but it is real life when one gets in touch with the Living Christ.

Others began to find the Lord as we continued to witness. My son and husband led their friends to the Lord. The district superintendent learned of this and, as he had already been seeking property in Belton for a future home mission project, urged us to begin services in spite of our limited time on furlough. This was the beginning of a new church.

There is nothing new about a church resulting from a home Bible class. I remember a man by the name of Cornelius in the 10th chapter of Acts. He was a Roman officer, a godly man who prayed and sought God often. By God's persuasion through an angel, Peter, the Bible teacher, entered the home of Cornelius and witnessed to him and to his relatives and friends whom Cornelius had invited in. The Holy Spirit fell on the group and the first Gentile church was born in a private home.

The Early Church was mainly home-centered. There were no church buildings yet, so the most convenient place to meet was in the homes. Many churches across our nation began as home Bible classes, and even today the home Bible class can be effective in church planting.

In addition, home Bible classes are being more and more used by the Holy Spirit for renewal of the church and its outreach. Many churches are discovering that the home Bible class opens a whole new means of evangelism. When people are exposed to personal study of the Bible they begin to discover the Living Word. Many misconceptions are cleared away. In teaching the Bible in the casual, open atmosphere of the living room, a new honesty before God's Word is quickened. The very structure of the home Bible class makes it conducive for presenting the gospel and makes it a fertile field for soul winning.

Recently in a home Bible class I was bringing the lesson to a conclusion when a new member of only two weeks broke into the discussion with tears streaming down her face and exclaimed, "I've never heard before how I could be saved. What am I supposed to do?" It was very natural to move into a soul-winning situation and explain the scriptures which created faith in Christ as her Savior. After praying for her and helping her to pray, Fran became a new creature in Christ that day. She is active in the group and growing in grace and in the knowledge of Christ.

Many are won after the class sessions are ended or before they leave the home. Others have been won in private conversations in their own homes. The Bible class teacher can sense the spiritual progress the class members are making and knows when one is ready to accept Christ. The teacher will make himself available and plan to "draw the net."

Not only do many discover the thrill of a newfound faith in Christ and experience its transforming power, but new friendships develop and grow among members. There is a trust and confidence in one another and a deep spiritual *koinonia* is released through the Holy Spirit.

There are many Christians in the church who have never discovered what God's Word really says. They have listened to pastors and Sunday school teachers, but have never delved into the Bible for themselves. In a home Bible class they will have a new discovery of the Bible. It will come alive and the fresh warmth of its meaning will touch areas in their lives that have never been explored or developed.

There are *advantages of group study:*

1. Being part of a Bible study class *helps one to develop a consistent pattern of study.*

A few months ago I was praying with a lady at the altar. She had not been a Christian very long and seemed to be confused about her relationship with Christ. I questioned her about her devotional life. She told me that when she picked up the Bible to read it she just skipped around until she found something that looked interesting. I explained to her the importance of systematic reading and study of God's Word. Since then she has been in one of my classes and is making real spiritual progress as she follows a regular pattern of Bible study.

2. In a home Bible class *each member shares his own experiences in life in relation to the passage being studied.* The Holy Spirit makes an impact of the passage for others present.

One day we were studying a passage of scripture from Mark 8:36-37: "What shall it profit a man, if he shall gain the whole world, and lose his own soul? Or what shall a man give in exchange for his soul?" A lady spoke up, "I've been thinking about this verse and thinking about all the things in my life I need to drop off or I'll be giving them in exchange for my own soul." She began to enumerate the things that were hindering her relationship with Christ. Everyone felt the impact of the scripture.

3. Being in a home Bible class *gives one an opportunity to test his own understanding of the text.*

It is surprising to find how many people read between the lines or read something into the Word that really isn't there. Members check each other on the basis of the passage when they study together.

4. When studying the Bible together as a group *one becomes accustomed to speaking of his relationship to God naturally and freely.*

In other settings one will more freely share what God means to him and witnessing will become natural.

5. After studying in a group *the individual spontaneously begins to search the Scriptures.* A habit pattern develops which remains with him throughout life.

II

Who For?

If we are going to see a genuine renewal of the church, the personal study of God's Word must be paramount, for the power of renewal is in the Word. Where two or three or more gather together to study the Bible with the Holy Spirit as the Teacher, the Word becomes "quick, and powerful, and sharper than any twoedged sword." The Word becomes alive and becomes the Word made flesh.

The home Bible class appeals to many people because there is provision for dialogue instead of monologue. There is opportunity for conversation, fellowship, communication and sharing of experiences. Doubts can be made known and answers sought. The home Bible class is a warmhearted situation in which God can work in the hearts and lives of the members.

There are different kinds of home Bible classes. The kind of class you form or teach should depend upon your aim.

1. You may want to form a class *for Christians* who have never really studied the Bible very much and feel a need to know it better. There are many, many Christians

who have never really studied God's Word for themselves, but have depended upon others to communicate the Word to them. They have never discovered the power in the Word that produces growth when one is directly involved with its text. In a stimulating group study the Word becomes alive in a way they have never before experienced.

Elton Trueblood, in his book *Your Other Vocation,* speaks about the thousands of men and women who have been in a Sunday school class for years without ever earnestly studying a single book of the Bible as a book. Dr. Trueblood feels that a "completely new pleasure in study would come to many Christians if they were to take a single book, such as the Gospel According to Luke, study its origin, it documentary background, its relation to the other Gospels, its probable authorship, its relation to the Book of Acts, and its unique character. There is no reason why thoughtful and reverent adults should not engage in such study."[10]

Many Christians have an unstable Christian experience because of a lack of discipline in their devotional lives. They have never developed "inner braces for the many outward pressures." In a home Bible class, members are encouraged to adopt some disciplines by which their lives can be changed. The key to growth in the life of the Spirit is discipline. Some of the following disciplines have been accepted in groups: regular attendance at the Sunday services, a period of daily reading of the Bible and prayer, family devotions, grace at meals, tithing one's income and time. These disciplines vary from group to group, for every group grows at a different pace.

2. You may want to form a class *for new Christians* who need to discover God's Word to help them in meaning-

10. Elton Trueblood, *Your Other Vocation* (New York: Harper and Row, Publishers, 1952), p. 113.

ful Christian living. This can be an exciting type of home Bible class. It is thrilling to see new Christians grow in grace and become "rooted and grounded in Christ" and established in God's Word. This type of class provides an excellent opportunity to lead new Christians into the deeper life of heart holiness.

3. You may want to form a class *for people who are unsaved,* who have totally bypassed the church, but who are searching for inner peace. This type of class is strictly evangelistic. There are some people who may never be willing to attend church. We must find other means of communicating the truth to them. A lot of people are willing to study something who would not be caught dead in a church service. The home Bible class is one of the most widely accepted settings for teaching biblical truth. Often these individuals will follow a spiritual leader to a church home after they have come in contact with the Living Christ.

The class members in an evangelistic home Bible class may represent various backgrounds, different denominations, and different opinions. But we must always remember that they all have a common need of knowing Christ. The group may consist of distinctly different individuals whose only common interest is to find out what the Bible says. There may be those with or without a Christian background. Some may come from morally upright families, others may have had a rough background with adulterous associations.

The teacher and/or host must always be courteous and make the members feel at ease by showing acceptance and a vital, personal interest in each one. Love must be genuine and warm. As you focus your attention on members of the group, think of them as individuals with strengths, weaknesses, and varied interests who need to discover something of the riches and challenge of God's Word.

12

How to Get Started

When I first arrived for the home Bible class in Bethel's living room, there were five ladies present. They looked at me with a mixture of apprehension and expectancy. Bethel served coffee and donuts and we all got acquainted. The atmosphere became casual and relaxed. We began studying the Gospel of John. I could tell this was a new experience to most of them. They had never really been exposed to God's Word before.

The children were in the playroom in the basement, but every so often one of them would come up crying or complaining or just interrupting. Bethel realized this could not be an ideal situation, so the following week other arrangements were made. The Bible study group met at a different apartment and the children stayed at Bethel's playroom with a competent baby-sitter. This helped the mothers to relax and to feel free from interruptions.

The group began to grow. Bethel took care of all the details—invitations, baby-sitter, refreshments and location (using different apartments). We had a time of warm fellowship. The group sat around in the living room, some on the floor, with Bibles opened on their laps, eager to be fed with the Bread of Life. There were 10 and 12 and sometimes 15 in our group—Methodists, Presbyterians, Lutherans, Pentecostals, Nazarenes, Catholics, and non-church attenders. There we were around the Word of God —sharing our deep needs, our spiritual progress, sensing the Holy Spirit revealing Christ to hungry hearts. These were precious moments. Weeks and months went by and different ones came to a personal faith in Christ. We could see the growth in spiritual perception and understanding of the Word. The Holy Spirit was present to teach us.

We studied the Gospel of John, the First Epistle of John, the Epistle of James. We took time to discuss various subjects and to search the Word for answers to questions and problems. We discussed: the work of the Holy Spirit, the gifts of the Spirit, Satanism and demon worship, the various cults, and the person and work of Christ.

Some of the ladies moved away, some had their work schedules changed, but new ones have joined the group and, after three years, the home Bible class is still vital and alive today under Bethel's continued leadership.

Perhaps you would like to see a home Bible class in your neighborhood but do not feel that you would be able to teach it. If you would speak to your pastor and express your desire to host a group, he would undoubtedly provide a teacher for you or at least have someone to get the group started for you.

The following are *suggestions* for getting a home Bible class *started:*

1. *Sponsorship*

The home Bible class is more effective if it is sponsored by the church. Churches should get involved in and develop the program either as an evangelistic arm or a convert's class meeting. The pastor ought to be the key promotor. Leaders can be trained by him or by some other spiritual Bible teacher in the church. The most vital and enthusiastic thrust with the home Bible class will always work from within the church outward. There will be a significant spiritual impact on the life of the whole church. When the church has taken the initiative and organized classes, there is no danger of a splinter group that breeds heresies. Churches that back the program and encourage home Bible classes meet with exciting success.

The home Bible class, however, should not become simply a means to recruit members. The individual members should feel welcome, but not obligated to join the sponsoring church. Converts should be encouraged to join a church that will foster their spiritual growth.

2. *Host or Hostess*

It is surprising how many people respond to an invitation to attend a Bible study group. People are really hungry for God's Word. As a host or hostess, it would be well to survey the area where you live, then invite your friends and neighbors with a printed invitation extended well ahead of the meeting. Follow up with a telephone reminder a day or so before the class begins. Do not make your friends feel that you are having a Bible study group for their benefit only. Let them know that you yourself feel the need of it. Help the group to feel that this is "their study" rather than "your" Bible study class.

Invitations to a study of four or six meetings which have a specific objective and topic make a good start for a home Bible class. Often people who are unfamiliar with a home Bible class will respond more favorably to discussing a variety of topics such as: "What is the Christian life?" "What is God like?" "Who was Jesus Christ?" "How can Jesus be made Lord of our lives?" "What is sin?" "What does it mean to believe?" etc. Then as the group continues to meet they will indicate their interest in the Bible and the study of a book in the Bible would be in order. You may want to choose various emphases which may be studied in individual books of the Bible such as: "Jesus as the Son of God" in the Gospel of John; "Jesus as a Man" in the Gospel of Mark; "Practical Christianity" in the Epistle of James; "Christian fellowship" in 1 John.

If you host a home Bible class, your responsibility would be to arrange for a place to have the Bible study, preferably a home that is adequate for the needs of the group. You would make provision for child care and arrange for someone to provide light refreshments. See that new people are introduced to the group and that a relaxed atmosphere prevails. The host, however, must be discreet and recognize that his responsibility ends when the teacher begins. There may be times when your well-placed question may stimulate discussion, but do not try to impress the group by your mature Christian experience.

3. *Number in Group and Time and Length of Meeting.*

If you have a class of unsaved people, limit the number of Christians that attend the class. Many times unbelievers feel outnumbered, stifled or embarrassed by their spiritual illiteracy. They resent the display of knowledge by others. A good ratio is about six to eight non-Christians to two or three Christians. A larger number of Christians than this will keep many of the group from taking part in the discussion.

The best promotion for your class is an enthusiastic member. Be willing to start with two or three. Christ has promised to be in the midst of two or three that are gathered in His Name. If you start with a small number of people and they enjoy the class, the group will grow naturally.

They will bring their friends. I have noticed that the openness of the group and the discussion are somewhat restricted when the group goes over 12 in attendance. There is more vigorous and meaningful discussion if the group is about 8 to 10.

It is wise to start a group experimentally with a time limit specified. Many people will accept a shorter commitment who would never consider a long one. Short-term classes are more attractive to the unsaved. Often, however, they later become permanent by mutual agreement and many times become so large that it is well to divide into two or more groups.

As to an appropriate time—morning, afternoon, and evening classes are all effective for Bible study groups. The daytime is preferable for a group of women because children are in school. However, couples, working women, and professional people are attracted to the evening classes. Let the group you are seeking to reach determine the time of your home Bible class. Remember there will still be some scheduling problems, but don't let this keep you from starting a group.

4. *Provision for Child Care*

Baby-sitting must be arranged ahead of time or mothers and couples will not attend. Providing a play area at a nearby house with a competent baby-sitter is very effective. Mothers feel relaxed and pleased to have an hour away from the children in a warmhearted social situation. Children begin to look forward to this time when they can be together.

It may be possible to use church facilities and hire the nursery attendants. Usually the parents involved want to contribute toward the expenses of a baby-sitter. Sometimes it is possible to find a baby-sitter who would volunteer to do the baby-sitting as a service to the church or to the group.

5. *Refreshments*

It is good to spend some time socializing just to get acquainted and feel at ease with one another. Simple refreshments encourage a friendly atmosphere. Some groups prefer to have the coffee and donuts before the lesson— this gives time for latecomers to arrive and not disturb the session after it gets started. It also puts the group at ease. Some groups prefer the refreshments at the close so that they can continue with personal interaction and warm fellowship. The class members feel free to ask questions and to talk frankly about spiritual things. I have found that morning groups seem to prefer the coffee time before the class begins, and evening classes prefer the refreshments at the close of the Bible study.

The refreshment time need not detract from the study period. Drinks and food should not be elaborate or costly, but should be kept simple. Let the refreshment time fit naturally and unobtrusively into the overall purpose and work of the class. Different ones in the group may volunteer to bring the refreshments from time to time.

13

What About the Leader?

Your spiritual life as a leader or teacher of a home Bible class is of utmost importance. The most important preparation for teaching is your personal relationship with God and your knowledge of His Word. Only as you are endued with God's Holy Spirit can you be a channel for His working in the group. Ask God to intensify a hunger for His Word. Always show full confidence in the Bible. Your respect for the authority of God's Word will be contagious. He will work through the Scriptures which you teach. Aim to have a Christ-centered group. Let the Spirit of Christ prevail in the class.

Always have a well-prayed-over lesson. As you study the lesson, take it before the Lord and seek His help in making the truths plain. Pray that your own eyes may be opened to see Him clearly. In prayer, mention each class member by name. Pray much for yourself and ask the Lord to show you any inconsistencies and weaknesses in your life of which you might not be aware and which might keep the group from believing what you say. Remember, in spiritual matters you cannot take someone where you have not been yourself. As you prepare for your classes you will find that you will grow spiritually yourself. Pray that God will help you make your Bible studies enjoyable and help you create a climate for learning. Pray that the class will be free, open, spontaneous, and vigorous.

Always be well prepared. This will help you to maintain poise and confidence, and you will feel a greater freedom and liberty as you speak. There may be times when questions arise that you cannot answer. Never feel that questions raised by members of the class are a threat to your spiritual insight or intellect. Don't expect to know all the answers all the time. Let the class know, however, that you do have the "Answer Book" in God's Word and that you will try to find an answer for the next session. Take your place in the group as "one who is learning more about Jesus Christ" and begin to identify with them.

Many answers may be found in a Bible dictionary, commentary, or concordance in your private study at home. Let the group know what source you have used to help illuminate the Word to your heart and mind. Always use God's Word, rather than your own opinion or experience, as the basis for all answers. If you are honest and humble, you too will discover many new truths along with the group.

Do not choose study materials at random. Work with your pastor regarding materials. Subject matter can easily be chosen that is divisive and harmful to the very unity it is supposed to help build. It is important that study materials have church approval.

Be appreciative of all that group members contribute. Your attitude will be one of the significant factors in determining the spirit and tone of the group. Your love and openness toward individuals in the group will be contagious. If you show a relaxed attitude and genuine enjoyment of the discussion, it will spread to every group member. Teaching will become easier as you concentrate on others' needs and set about communicating the life-changing principles of the Word.

Teacher Checkup

1. Is my speaking voice distinct, convincing, easy to hear?

2. Do I dress attractively and neatly, but in a way that won't detract attention from what I say? Mrs. G. B. Williamson says: "Seek to be attractive but not an attraction."

3. Is my manner of presentation friendly, unstilted, pleasant?

4. Do I allow freedom of expression by others in the group, yet keep the group on the subject?

5. Am I enthusiastic, vibrant, and joyful? Is there a glow and radiance about my life?

6. Do I have a good sense of humor? This can be a valuable asset in leadership but should never be at the expense of any individual in the class. It can often relieve the tension of embarrassment or disagreement.

7. Am I emotionally mature? Can I view myself objectively and profit from any remarks that are made if my views are questioned or criticized?

8. Do I learn the names of my class members quickly? (Remember, the sweetest sound to one's ears is his own name.)

9. Am I offensive in any way? (Keep breath mints handy . . . after speaking for a while your breath may need it. People will be talking to you after class, so don't take chances! If you are tense you may tend to perspire more. Be sure your deodorant is effective.)

10. Do I reflect the Spirit of Christ in my personality? Remember, our lives are of value only as Christ is in us.

14

How to Conduct the Class

There is no set procedure for conducting a successful class. As you lead the group under the direction of the Holy Spirit, He will provide you with your own approach adapted to the needs of your particular group.

Your first class may be the most difficult as you face a room full of strange faces. Some may seem to be apprehensive. Others will look at you expectantly. Smile, be warm, put them at ease. The host or hostess should introduce you to the group and introduce the class members to you. If they fail to do so you may say, "Let's get acquainted before we begin." Introduce yourself and have each one give his or her name. Express your excitement about the class. Be prepared to lead this first meeting in a way that the group will immediately feel it was a profitable experience.

Start with prayer at the beginning of each class. Acknowledge your dependence upon the Holy Spirit's guidance and illumination of each truth. Be relaxed in your own attitude and manner. Remember that the class is not yours but the Lord's, so don't get tense!

Have the Bible chapter you are studying read aloud by paragraphs or thought units—not verse by verse. Do not call on specific people to read. Someone may not read very well and this will embarrass him. There will be those in the group who do read well and will volunteer. It is not necessary for everyone to read aloud, or for each to read an equal amount.

The reading of the passage may be done in two ways: (1) Read the whole chapter aloud before discussing the questions paragraph by paragraph. Or (2) read a paragraph or section aloud and discuss that portion before reading the next portion. This latter method is helpful in those chapters where there is little connection between the paragraphs or larger sections.

Try to stick to the Bible passage under discussion. Discover all that you can from the section you are studying without moving around to other books of the Bible in cross references. This means that the person new to the Bible will not needlessly be confused, and you will avoid the danger of taking portions out of context.

You may need to lay the scene for the lesson with geographical and historical data. The Bible portion to be studied must be shown to have relevance. Keep in mind that the Bible is a channel for present-day experience with God. In it we find not truth about God, but God himself.

In order to be effective, you must discover how to use dialogue effectively. Lecturing is not the most important method. Dialogue must be discovered where mutual challenge takes place. Try to draw out every person in the group so that there is full participation. When several people share their ideas, new ideas are born. Participation stimulates thinking. It initiates the search for deep truths. Make it clear that each one has something unique to contribute to the discussion, something that no one else can make.

An openness of the group will come if you as the teacher open up to God and are honest with Him. For the Word to so permeate our experience, we have to open up our own lives. We have to open up to ourselves and consciously explore the harmony or disharmony of our experience with God's Word. We have to open ourselves to one another, to be willing to share not only our experience with Christ, but also our needs and failures.

Openness and meaningful sharing do not always come quickly or easily. But they do come! They come when the teacher resists taking an authoritarian role and instead stimulates his class members to discover that God's Word speaks for itself. They come when the teacher encourages a free and spontaneously developing discussion.

As we all come to the Word in the group and open our lives and allow the Holy Spirit to search us, we can respond to Him, and we will begin to grow spiritually. As we learn to share our thoughts and our experiences with each other, we come to know, to love, and to trust each other in Christ. It is then that we become a fellowship.

Let your class know that no one is ever changed unless he wants to be, and even then he is powerless without God's help. No truth is found unless it is sought. As you teach the Bible—teach it creatively, with challenge, with relationship to life, and with relevance. Taught this way, it will transform and promote spiritual growth. God's life-changing truth should be taught in a life-changing way.

The Nondenominational Class

Make clear at the beginning that the home Bible class is nondenominational. This helps when someone may try to push his pet doctrine. Each one must follow the Lord's leading regarding his choice of a church. The group must feel free from denominational obligations which the teacher might represent. However, many will follow a spiritual leader to a church home. The Spirit of Christ must always prevail in the Bible study group so that the church is built up and strengthened, not weakened and destroyed. A critical spirit will destroy the purpose of the classes.

No fellowship group should become a substitute for church attendance or church activity. Many individuals who have never belonged to a church find that their small-group experience leads directly into a commitment to the larger church body.

Handling Controversy and Irrelevant Issues

Many fear leading a Bible study class because discussion may get out of hand and they will not know how to handle controversial questions. Remember that differences of opinion can stimulate interest and thought by all members in the group. The teacher should aim to guide discussion rather than to stifle it. Teachers do not help class members by cutting off negative ideas or faulty impressions. A true corrective will come in the period of Bible study.

When controversy threatens to consume the class time, suggest that you wait until class is over, then those who want to continue the discussion may remain. I have found that going to lunch with two or three afterwards who were bothered by the discussion helped them to air their differences outside of the group and the Holy Spirit helped to explain the Scriptures personally to them.

Never allow vigorous debate in the group. If necessary, tactfully reiterate the rule that our basic purpose is to lift up Jesus Christ. Discussion is welcome but no arguments are permitted.

Sometimes an overtalkative person may try to dominate the group. The leader must politely steer the discussion away from the domineering individual back to the group. Help the group recognize the need for balanced participation.

Always listen courteously, but interrupt, if necessary, to keep a discussion relevant to the Word. If questions regarding doctrinal differences are brought up, say: "We realize these differences exist. I'll be glad to discuss them with you after class."

Deal with irrelevant issues by suggesting that the purpose of the study is to discover what is in the passage. Receive all participation warmly. Never bluntly reject what anyone says, even if you think the answer is incorrect. Ask in a friendly manner, "What do some of the rest of you think?" Or, "Is that what the Word actually says?" Allow the group to handle problems together. When the Holy Spirit is the Teacher, He wonderfully smooths out any controversial issues or irrelevant subjects and helps the leader maintain a unity and harmony in the group.

Participation

Another objection to being a leader is the problem of getting others to take part or to speak up. Usually after rapport within the group is established there is no difficulty in getting people to express themselves. Be sure you do not talk too much as the leader. Redirect some of the questions that are asked you back to the group. As the members of the group get to know each other, the discussion will move more freely.

The good leader will encourage the members of the class to take part, to express themselves, to ask questions, to answer one another's questions. The leader is to act as a moderator. He will be ready to move on to the next point, or to ask a leading question, or to keep the group on target.

Plan to divide the time into segments if need be: background, teaching and application, discussion. Be flexible! Each class progresses from meeting to meeting. But have a

73

plan. Impose a time limit on the length of your meeting. Usually 45 minutes to an hour is sufficient. It is always better to terminate a meeting while interest is high rather than to let it drift on until people get weary or bored. A good rule is to keep them longing rather than loathing!

15

Methods and Helps to Use

When the apostle Paul wrote to Timothy in his second letter, he reminded him that he was taught the Holy Scriptures. He said,

> From infancy you have known the holy Scriptures, which are able to make you wise for salvation through faith in Christ Jesus. All Scripture is God-breathed and is useful for teaching, rebuking, correcting and training in righteousness, so that the man of God may be thoroughly equipped for every good work (2 Tim. 3:15-17, NIV).

In the home Bible class we can experience the truth of these verses as we expose ourselves to God's Word and open our lives to God's scrutiny.

There are various methods of Bible study that are being used today in the home Bible class. As you lead the group under the direction of the Holy Spirit, He will provide you with your own approach, adapted to the needs of your particular group.

Let us look at some of the methods of Bible study.

1. *Inductive Bible Study*

An inductive Bible study is one of the most effective and stimulating methods of study. This method of study puts the accent on the direct, personal discovery of meanings in the Bible. The leader does not state the answers, but asks questions of the class members from the facts they observe and analyze in a given passage of scripture. This leads to the forming of a conclusion. For many the Bible becomes "alive" and meaningful. What is personally discovered is always more one's own than what is taught in lecture form. The discussion questions are based on the passage being studied, allowing the passage to speak for itself. The questions in inductive Bible study fall into three categories:

a. What does it say? (Fact)

b. What does it mean? (Interpretation)

c. What does it mean to me? (Application)

The teacher should be sufficiently familiar with the material and well enough prepared to steer the discussion. The answers to the questions should always center in the Word. The meaning of the passage will lead to the knowledge of the way God wants us to think and the way He expects us to live. The Christians at Berea were commended by Paul for examining "the Scriptures daily to see if these things were true" (Acts 17:11).

2. *Deductive Bible Study*

Deductive Bible study develops a systematic theology on the basis of various passages. It begins with a stated premise which serves as a filter through which biblical passages are studied. If the original premise is inaccurate the later deductions cannot be relied upon. In this method of study the Bible is often fractured into piecemeal proof-texting. It is often used by the cultists who freely quote the Bible but whose theology is foreign to the Word of God.

3. *The Springboard or Casual-Reading-and-Discussion Method*

The "springboard" is a popular approach to the Bible today in which the subject matter is analyzed from a textual point of view. The group shares their experiences and opinions after a casual reading of the Scriptures and shift to discussion of current issues. Such discussion often degenerates into discord over popular prejudices. In the springboard method there is no investigation of what the Bible says, no search for truth, no in-depth study, no emphasis on the importance of God's Word being inspired.

4. *The Lecture Method*

Lecturing is simply a process of teaching in which the leader communicates information, facts, or concepts. In using the lecture method the teacher must have the ability to take a passage of scripture and communicate information about the passage in such a way that it becomes a living, relevant picture. Sermons are often of this type. They challenge, instruct, exhort, and call for a decision.

An overemphasis on one-way communication, however, violates some of the basic principles of teaching. When an individual is involved and motivated in group participation, he learns to become an independent investigator of the Word of God. Individuals whose only Christian teaching is secondhand, from listening to pastors and teachers, often lack an enthusiasm for the Word. They accept the teacher as the final authority for truth. The Bible is the authority; the teacher is only the agent through whom the Word is communicated.

If you use the lecture method, try combining the lecture with group involvement methods such as discussion, questions and answers, and the expression of reactions. This will allow for feedback. It might also help to give the class members a mimeographed outline or guide to follow while you speak.

5. *Rotation of Leader*

Some Bible study groups rotate the leadership of the discussion weekly and use Bible study guides. One may find a number of different study guides on various books of the Bible which may be purchased at Bible bookstores. At the back of this book is such a guide for studying Ephesians. The leader guides the group through the Bible passage by asking questions from the study guide. This type of class centers around seeking and sharing experiences rather than a teacher-pupil arrangement. The Bible is discussed in simple language and in terms of everyday living. Truth is shared rather than taught.

6. *Study Bibles*

With the introduction of many new versions in modern language, it is becoming increasingly easy for the unlearned and the new convert to read and understand the Bible. During the Reformation the laity received the Bible in their everyday language. They could read it and understand it in terms of life.

During the early years of my missionary career in Haiti, the American Bible Society had the New Testament translated and printed in Creole, the language of the people. In our missionary work we put a great emphasis on literacy classes, teaching adults and children to read. It was thrilling to see the Haitian people begin to read God's Word for themselves in their own language which spoke directly to their hearts. This was one of the keys to the revival and tremendous growth which we witnessed during those years.

New converts need to discover the Bible for itself. The Bible will speak for itself! It can be used by the Holy Spirit to reach the heart. Discovery in the Bible under the impact of the Holy Spirit produces exciting experiences in the home Bible class.

It is recommended that everyone in the class have at least one recent translation of the Bible. In fact, in a neighborhood Bible class among persons who are unfamiliar with the teaching of the Bible, it is better to use only one translation, not a variety—either *Today's English Version* or the *New International Version* is recommended. The American Bible Society has printed the TEV in a paperback edition entitled *Good News for Modern Man* which may be purchased cheaply. The NIV is also available in paperback. I have found it helpful to give copies of an inexpensive paperback of a recent translation to class members, then make reference to passages by giving the page number. This saves embarrassment in finding the passage for those who are unfamiliar with the Bible.

For a study group composed of mature Christians the use of many different translations opens the way for new insights into biblical truth.

The King James Version is good Shakespearean English, and though its literary quality is unsurpassed, the real meaning of many words has changed in 400 years. To a person unfamiliar with the Bible, reading becomes heavy and difficult and soon they set it aside thinking, "I can't understand the Bible very well."

There are many other helpful translations available: the *New American Standard Bible,* the Phillips translation, the Berkeley Version, the *Twentieth Century New Testament,* the *Amplified Bible,* and others.

Some groups prefer to use *The Living Bible,* which is

very helpful to many because of its contemporary language. If you do use *The Living Bible,* explain that it is a paraphrase, and not a completely accurate translation.

7. *Commentaries and Bible Handbooks*

Many different commentaries are available, and it is wise to ask your pastor's help in selecting those that would be helpful in your personal study and preparation as a leader. Never take the commentaries or Bible handbooks to the class. They have no place in a group study. The Scriptures should be the final authority. The Bible is our textbook and it is supreme. Always remember that the group is not meeting together to share opinions based on a favorite author or pastor or commentary. The aim is to discover what the Bible says and to study it without denominational dogma. Avoid theologically oriented terminology. Any words or expressions not understood should be explained.

*   *   *

Always lift up Jesus Christ so that He will be seen as the only Savior. He is continually drawing men to himself. Trust Him to lead you to those in whose lives He is or will be working. As the Living Presence becomes real and creative and empowering in the lives of the group members, there will inevitably be renewal that will come to the church.

Bibliography

Small Groups

Howard, Walden, comp. *Groups That Work.* Grand Rapids: Zondervan Publishing House, 1967.

Howe, Reuel L. *The Miracle of Dialogue.* New York: The Seabury Press, 1963.

McLaughlin, Raymond. *Communication for the Church.* Grand Rapids: Zondervan Publishing House, 1968.

Mowrer, O. Hobart. *The New Group Therapy.* New York: Van Nostrand Reinhold Company, 1964.

Powell, S. J. *Why Am I Afraid to Tell You Who I Am?* Niles, Ill.: Argus Communications, 1969.

Richards, Lawrence O. *69 Ways to Start a Study Group.* Grand Rapids: Zondervan Publishing House, 1968.

Rogers, Carl R. *Carl Rogers on Encounter Groups.* New York: Harper and Row, Publishers, 1970.

Shepherd, Clovis R. *Small Groups, Some Sociological Perspectives.* Scranton, Pa.: Chandler Publishing Co., 1964.

Trueblood, Elton. *Your Other Vocation.* New York: Harper and Row, Publishers, 1952.

———. *The Company of the Committed.* New York: Harper and Row, Publishers, 1961.

Prayer Groups

Rinker, Rosalind. *Prayer: Conversing with God.* Grand Rapids: Zondervan Publishing House, 1959.

———. *Communicating Love Through Prayer.* Grand Rapids: Zondervan Publishing House, 1966.

———. *Praying Together,* Grand Rapids: Zondervan Publishing House, 1968.

Bible Study

Gangel, Kenneth. *24 Ways to Improve Your Teaching.* Wheaton, Ill.: Victor Books, 1974.

Nyquist, James F. *Leading Bible Discussions.* Downers Grove, Ill.: InterVarsity Press, 1967.

Richards, Lawrence O. *Creative Bible Teaching.* Chicago: Moody Press, 1970.

Wollen, Albert J. *How to Conduct Home Bible Classes.* Wheaton, Ill.: Scripture Press Publications, Inc., 1969.

The Epistle of Paul
to the
EPHESIANS

A Bible Study Guide
by
Marion K. Rich

A Supplement to
Discovery—The Art of Leading Small Groups

To the Leader

It is recommended that in using this study guide one of the newer versions of the Bible be used—preferably *Today's English Version* (*Good News Bible*, American Bible Society) or the *New International Version* (Zondervan Publishing House). The version used in the scripture quotes herein is the TEV unless otherwise indicated.

This study may be used for groups of non-Christians as an evangelistic outreach. Key passages are given in the "Teacher's Directives," which may be used to present the way of salvation.

This guide may also be used for groups of new converts or Christians who need to become established in Christ or led into a deeper experience of heart holiness. These passages are also indicated in the "Teacher's Directives."

Introduction to Ephesians

The Author—The apostle Paul wrote the book of Ephesians as a letter to the church at Ephesus about A.D. 61 or 62. Paul was a prisoner at Rome at the time. It is believed that this letter was not written to the church at Ephesus only, but was a kind of circular letter sent first to Ephesus, then afterwards to the various neighboring churches of Asia Minor. The letter was written near the close of Paul's four years' imprisonment. Because he probably had ample time for much prayer and meditation, this letter gives a more mature reflection on God's great eternal purposes for the human race.

Background—For a background in the Scriptures of Paul's remarkable labors at Ephesus, it is recommended that you read Acts 18 and 19.

The city of Ephesus was a city in Asia Minor, and at one time the metropolis of that part of the world. It was a busy center of commerce, the highway into Asia from Rome. Ephesus was notorious for its luxury and permissiveness. Sorcery or magic was very common. Religion and superstition were a compound of the East and the West. Diana, or Artemis, a goddess of the West, was the chief object of worship, but the style of her worship had in it much of Oriental mystery.

In the Book of Acts we read that in Ephesus Paul was helped by Aquila and Priscilla, and by Apollos. Paul was given a special manifestation of supernatural power and many miracles were wrought through him. The first scene of his preaching was the synagogue, but his reception there was so unfavorable that he had to leave it. His success among the Gentiles was much greater than among the Jews. The power of God's Word was so great that it even subdued those who had become rich by lucrative sin. Many exorcists and persons who practiced magical arts became converts to Christ as a result of the power given to Paul to cast out evil spirits. They proved their sincerity by burning their books and abandoning forever a business which might have enriched them in this world, but would have ruined their souls. A church in Ephesus such as this that had surrendered so much for Christ could not but be dear to Paul.

Contents—The subject of Paul's letter to the Ephesians has been stated as, "The believer's place in Christ and Christ's place in the believer." In Ephesians we find Paul's concern with unity—unity between man and God, and unity between Jew and Gentile. We also find here God's highest thought for His Church as an instrument of reconciliation and unity. The Book of Ephesians is often referred to as "The Epistle of Christian Maturity."

Ephesians is divided into two sections (1) Doctrinal, chapters 1—3, and (2) Practical, chapters 4—8.

CHAPTER 1

Spiritual Blessings in Christ

Begin by having different ones in the group read the chapter by paragraphs. The discussion questions are designed to help members of the group discover for themselves some basic truths about living the Christian life.

Discussion Questions	Teacher's Commentary and Directives
Verses 1-2	Verses 1-2
How does Paul describe himself?	Paul describes himself as an apostle of Jesus Christ, which literally means "sent forth by Christ." Paul was personally commissioned by Christ on the Damascus Road to preach the gospel (cf. Acts 26:15-19; Gal. 1:11-17).
To whom did Paul write this letter?	"To God's people . . . those who are faithful in their life in Christ Jesus." "Faithful" may mean believers or those who have faith, those who have received Christ as Savior.
	(Teacher, explain that this does not come by one's own personal efforts but comes only by willingly and knowingly surrendering one's life to God.)
What is given by God and Christ?	"Grace and peace." These are like twin sisters. Grace is "free, undeserved mercy" and is the only foundation of true peace —whether peace with God, peace with our fellowman, or peace of conscience. Peace is that state of deep satisfaction and settledness. This letter has often been called "The Epistle of Grace" because the letter is so full of the subject.

Discussion Questions	Teacher's Commentary and Directives
	Note: In most of Paul's letters he begins with a threefold greeting which was common to first-century Christians. In his salutations he tells who wrote the letter, to whom he was writing, and then gives a benediction.

Verses 3-5

What has been given to every true Christian, according to the doxology of verse 3?

Are temporal blessings and spiritual blessings related?

Notice the phrase:
  "heavenly world"
    (TEV)
  "heavenly realms"
    (NIV)
  "heavenly places"
    (KJV)
To what does Paul refer by this phrase?

In v. 4 Paul tells us why we have been chosen in Christ. Explain.

When did God decide this plan for perfecting His people? (v. 4).

What was included in God's predestination? (v. 5).

Verses 3-5

Paul begins with praise to God for the blessings and gifts that come as a result of our union with Christ. All the benefits that come to us, either material or spiritual, are attributed to God.

This expression is found five times in Ephesians. It refers to the place where believers can enjoy a deep fellowship with Christ. The inner life of man in Christ has been invaded by the power of heaven. The Christian is in the world but not of the world (cf. John 17:13-16). In spirit the believer is lifted above the temporal or the earthly.

"So that we would be holy and without fault before him." Holy refers to the inner spiritual quality. Without blame refers to the outer conduct of our lives.

"Before the world was made." The work of redemption was planned and its details arranged from all eternity.

"Through Jesus Christ he would bring us to himself as his sons" or "He predestined us to be adopted as sons" (NIV).

Discussion Questions	Teacher's Commentary and Directives
	Note that there are two aspects of sonship.
	(1) Through a heavenly birth we partake of the divine nature. Jesus spoke about the necessity of the new birth to Nicodemus in John 3:3—"No one can see the Kingdom of God unless he is born again."
	(2) Through adoption. Paul uses this idea five times in his letters. It suggests a legal transaction which brings us into the full privileges of the family. The Christian is placed in the position of a full-grown son, which makes him a full heir; a "joint heir with Jesus Christ."
	(Teacher, use this opportunity to explain what happens when one becomes a child of God. Lay a foundation for the way of salvation and trust the Holy Spirit to begin working in individual hearts.)
Verses 6-10	**Verses 6-10**
Note how each section ends with praise.	
For what does Paul say that we should praise God? (v. 6).	"Let us praise God for his glorious grace." Paul is saying that God has "treated us graciously." God's gift of salvation is central. In the gift of His Son the gift of grace becomes ours. No other way can we know God's redeeming grace apart from Christ.
What is the great price paid for the forgiveness of our sins? (v. 7).	The blessings referred to in v. 3 are now specified: "By the death of Christ we are set free." We are redeemed—"bought back by payment of a ransom." Our redemption is through the blood of Christ.

Discussion Questions	Teacher's Commentary and Directives
	(Teacher, explain here what the believer experiences when he is saved. There is release, freedom from the guilt of our transgressions. The Psalmist said, "As far as the east is from the west, so far hath he removed our transgressions from us.")
In v. 8 we see two of God's attributes that are illuminated by His grace. What are they?	"Wisdom and insight" or understanding. The height of wisdom is shown in God's way of making His grace abound toward us.
What is this secret plan in vv. 9 and 10?	"He will bring all creation together with Christ as head." God will complete His plan when the time is ripe. Things are moving towards it, and one day it will be wholly realized. Paul here envisions the final victory of the Kingdom.

Verses 11-14

Verses 11-14

Does God's plan for our lives also secure the future?

Salvation insures a rich, spiritual inheritance. Not only did we, in vital union with Christ, receive such blessings as redemption, forgiveness of sin, and spiritual illumination, but also the right to future glory was bestowed upon us. "We were made heirs." Certain blessings are bestowed upon us here and now, others in the hereafter.

To whom might Paul be referring in v. 12 by the clause: "The first to hope in Christ"?

Verse 12: The Jews were the chosen of God not for personal privilege but for salvation purposes. Paul makes it plain that the Jews, too, must come to Christ for salvation in order to share in this inheritance.

Discussion Questions	Teacher's Commentary and Directives
How should the knowledge of such an inheritance cause us to live? (v. 12).	"To the praise of God's glory" (v. 12). Note: In the Westminster Catechism it reads that "Man's chief end is to glorify God, and to enjoy Him forever."
In what ways can man glorify God?	
When one really hears the gospel message and believes it, what does God do for him? (v. 13).	Verse 13: "God puts his stamp of ownership on you by giving you the Holy Spirit." *(Teacher, explain that when one is genuinely born of the Spirit and raised to newness of life in Christ, the Holy Spirit gives an assurance within the heart. Entrance of the Holy Spirit into the life through the new birth marks one as belonging to God. It is a legal act of God, not just an emotional experience.)*
What part in our inheritance does the Holy Spirit have? (v. 14).	Verse 14: "The Spirit is the guarantee that we shall receive what God has promised."
How does one get that seal, that inner assurance?	Not as the result of self-searching but by a living faith in Christ.

Paul's Prayer (1:15-23)

In verses 3-14 we read of Paul's testimony of praise to God for spiritual blessings in Christ. In this section (15-23) we have Paul's intercession for God's people in order that they might know the extent of their blessings in Christ. The believer who earnestly desires to mature and grow in Christ must cultivate a heart of praise and pray for a spirit of wisdom.

Discussion Questions	Teacher's Commentary and Directives

Verses 15-23

Verses 15-23

What are some causes of deficiency in the areas of prayer and praise in the Christian community today?

Busyness, self-sufficiency, lack of spiritual perception, emphasis on materialism and secularism, social pressures, etc. These may be some causes for the lack of prayer and praise among Christians today.

What are the characteristics of the Ephesian Christians which are revealed in v. 15?

They had faith in the Lord Jesus, and love for all God's people.
(Explain how faith in Christ brings about a divine love in the heart—cf. Rom. 5:5.)

What does v. 16 reveal about the apostle Paul?

He is a man of prayer.
He thanks God for them continuously.
He prays for them.

(Teacher, you may want to elaborate on the ingredients in Paul's prayer: thanksgiving, praise, and intercession.)

How is God identified in v. 17?

The terms by which Paul calls on God are always significant:
   "God of our Lord Jesus Christ."
   "Glorious Father" (the Father to whom the glory belongs).

What did Paul want the Christians to experience? (vv. 17-18).

The Holy Spirit, who would give them wisdom, revelation, knowledge, and understanding. Paul prays for their minds to be opened to see the light.

(Teacher, explain the blindness of one's heart before one comes to Christ who is the Light. Also emphasize the importance of seeking more knowledge even after we have been saved and sealed by the Holy Spirit. A growing knowledge is a healthful feature of the Christian life.)

91

Discussion Questions	Teacher's Commentary and Directives

In vv. 19 and 20 Paul speaks about the "incomparably great power for us who believe" and mentions that this is the same power which raised Christ from the dead. In what ways does this power work in the believer's transformation?

Paul often uses the figure of "Christ's resurrection power" at work in the believer who was dead in sins. This mighty power works in them the needed transformation.

(Teacher, here is an opportunity to point out the change that takes place in one who accepts Christ. He becomes "a new creature—old things are passed away and all things are become new" [cf. 2 Cor. 5:17]. Explain also how this power is needed daily to live victoriously.)

How does the exaltation of Christ in vv. 21-23 impress you?

How great is the one who empowers us?

Verse 21—note the preeminence of Christ's name which is to be eternal. In human history we find no name worthy to be coupled with His name. There is power in Christ's Name (cf. Acts 2:21; 4:12; Phil. 2:9-11).

Verse 22—"God put all things under Christ's feet." Christ has the whole creation at His disposal.

Verse 23—The gift of Christ to the Church is the gift of One who has sovereign authority over all things. The Church is Christ's body in a real, spiritual sense. He is the Head, His people the members. He dwells in the Church as life dwells in a living body—strengthening, feeding, beautifying, calming with peace, and brightening with His Holiness.

Conclusion

Teacher, in concluding this first chapter, emphasize again the plan of salvation.

92

God the Father planned our salvation (1:4-6).

His Son paid for it by His death (1:7-12).

The Holy Spirit applies it to one's heart and life (1:13-14).

Have class members underline key words and phrases. Discuss them: "spiritual blessings," "in the heavenlies," "God chose us," "riches of his grace," "in Christ."

For a class of more mature Christians you may want to discuss the subjects of sovereign election and predestination. It is better not to go too deeply into these terms with people who are unfamiliar with the Scriptures. Keep the discussion on a level where all may understand.

◆ ◆ ◆

CHAPTER 2

From Death to Life

This chapter may be studied in two units—vv. 1-10, then vv. 11-22. In chapter 1, Paul talks about the divine power of Christ and wants us to know how rich we are in Christ. In chapter 2, he shows the working of that same power in the believer's life and appeals to Christians to remember their lost condition before they were saved.

Discussion Questions	Teacher's Commentary and Directives
Verses 1-10	Verses 1-10
What are some of the characteristics of the old life of sin? (vv. 1-3).	(1) Spiritually dead because of disobedience and sins.
	(2) Followed the ways of this world.
	(3) Obeyed the ruler of the kingdom of the air.
	(4) Gratified the cravings of the sinful nature.
	(5) By nature were objects of God's wrath.

Discussion Questions	Teacher's Commentary and Directives
	(Teacher, these verses can be mightily used by the Holy Spirit to help those who have not yet accepted Christ as their Savior to see their need of Him. Your own personal testimony of the change in your life may be effective here.)
Though some people may have high moral standards, if they are rejecting Christ as Savior to what class do they belong? (v. 2).	Paul speaks about the spirit of the ruler of the kingdom of the air (referring to Satan). This spirit is still at work and controls the people who disobey God.
What does it mean to "suffer God's wrath" or to be "objects of God's wrath?"	Persons without God in their pre-Christian state are committed to sin by nature or by their very being. We belonged to a race that incurred the wrath of God (cf. John 3:36; Rom. 1:18).
Notice the impact of the words "But God" in v. 4. How would you compare v. 1—"In the past you were spiritually dead" with v. 4— "But God's mercy is so abundant"?	Paul sketches the dark background of spiritual death, then gives a characterization of the new life in Christ. "But God" —God always makes a difference in the life. Love is the motive for His mercy. His love is the groundwork for our salvation. His mercy provided our Savior, the Lord Jesus.
What does the apostle reiterate again in v. 5 which he mentioned in v. 1? Why?	Paul emphasizes again the past life when we were "spiritually dead." He did not turn from us when we were deep in sin, but He began to influence us even when we were dead in sin. Notice His resurrection power—"He brought us to life with Christ." The new life in Christ is resurrection life!

Discussion Questions	Teacher's Commentary and Directives
To what is this experience attributed? (v. 5).	"It is by God's grace that you have been saved." Here again is unmerited favor—God's love poured out abundantly upon us.
In v. 6 Paul speaks of a place that every child of God occupies. What is this place?	"He raised us up with him to rule with him in the heavenly world" or "seated us with him in the heavenly realms" (NIV). Because of our union with Christ, we have a right to the kingdom of God where the privileges of heaven are ours and the fellowship and enjoyment of heaven are known. We live temporarily on earth as long as we remain in this body but our citizenship is in heaven.
Why did God demonstrate his grace? (v. 7).	That in the coming ages spiritually resurrected men will be an example. Through all generations men will know that God forgives the sins of the most sinful when they repent and believe in Christ.
In vv. 8 and 9, notice that Paul is repeating what he mentioned in v. 5. Here he expands the subject of salvation by faith.	On the part of God, salvation is by grace; on man's part it is through faith. Faith believes the good news of a free salvation through Christ and accepts Christ as Savior and Lord. It is not by good works that we earn the right to be delivered from sin and death.
What part does God have in our salvation? What is man's part?	*(Teacher, here is an excellent opportunity to make plain the way of salvation and to help those who are not saved to come to a decision today. Encourage them to put their faith and trust in Christ to save them. Pray much for the Holy Spirit to lead you. As you sense a responsiveness in those who need Christ, do not be afraid to draw the net.)*

Discussion Questions	Teacher's Commentary and Directives
What do we do when someone offers us a gift?	A gift is not ours until we receive it. We, too, must receive God's gift of salvation before we know we are saved. *(Teacher, emphasize that the "gift of God" is a free gift without money and without price. In many places of the New Testament, salvation is represented as a gift. Cf. John 3:15; 4:14; Rom. 6:23; 2 Cor. 9:15.)*
Paul makes it clear that we have no works of our own that we can offer God toward our salvation, but in v. 10 what does he say is the ultimate purpose of salvation which comes through the new birth?	The purpose of the new creation is to produce good works. We are not saved because of our good works, yet we are saved that we may perform good works for God's glory. The apostle James stresses the importance of good works being a result of our faith.

Verses 11-18 are a picture of the unbeliever—once alienated, now reconciled. This paragraph is about two kinds of alienations of Gentiles, (1) from Israel; (2) from God and Christ. Paul emphasizes the truth that there is no distinction between Jews and Gentiles to those who are in Christ. Both have been reconciled to God through Christ's death on the cross.

Discussion Questions	Teacher's Commentary and Directives
In v. 11 Paul exhorts us to remember what we were in the past.	In vv. 11 and 12 Paul describes their religious condition "apart from Christ," just as he had described their moral condition in vv. 1-3.
In v. 12, what are the five things said about the unregenerate? (You	Verse 12: (1) Apart from Christ (2) Foreigners

Discussion Questions	Teacher's Commentary and Directives

may need to explain the term "unregenerate" if there are those in the group who are unfamiliar with the gospel.)

(3) Did not belong to God's chosen people
(4) No part in the covenants
(5) Lived in this world without hope, without God

Verse 13—"But now." Here again is a dramatic transition. All is changed in Christ! How has this new and living way been opened to those who would receive it?

Verse 13—"Through the blood of Christ." The shed blood of Christ makes atonement for us. It cleanses from all sin. "It brings us near." Notice the new figure of speech that Paul uses here. He had been making a contrast between death and life. Now it is between distance and nearness. Both Jew and Gentile can be brought nearer to God and nearer to one another as a result of the sacrifice of Christ. When we are in Christ the great barriers are removed from our lives.

In vv. 14-17, Paul points out that Christ is not only our Peacemaker, but our Peace. There is peace not only between Jew and Gentile, but between God and both.

What has been broken down as a result of Christ's redemptive work?

He broke down the wall that separated Jews and Gentiles and that kept them enemies. Some writers feel that this may refer to the five-foot-high wall in the Temple area at Jerusalem which separated the Court of the Gentiles from the Court of the Jews. The penalty for a Gentile entering the Jews' court was death. (Note Paul's experience in Acts 21:26-29).

Discussion Questions	Teacher's Commentary and Directives
	Whatever divisions exist between the races and nations, Christ breaks down every barrier. The greatest triumph of the apostolic age was that it overcame the long-standing estrangement between Jew and Gentile and enabled them to become one in Christ. In order to have peace with God, we must have peace with one another.
In vv. 13, 16, and 18, what is the way to reconciliation?	Christ Jesus! He has done away with distance, division, and distinction.
What figures does Paul use to express the unity between Jewish and Gentile believers? (v. 19).	Verse 19—"Fellow citizens with God's people." "Members of the family of God."
In vv. 20-22, Paul uses other figures to set forth another aspect of our relationship in Christ. What are they?	Verses 20-22: "Built on the foundation." "Sacred temple of the Lord." "House where God lives through his Spirit." The Church of Christ consists of all people genuinely born again, cemented by the Holy Spirit to the one Foundation. It is a spiritual structure in which the power of God is manifested in the world.

◆   ◆   ◆

CHAPTER 3

Paul's Testimony and Prayer

Teacher, if you read carefully Acts 21:18-36 you will have an excellent background to Eph. 3:1-13. Paul writes this letter from a prison in Rome. The occasion for the arrest was a false charge about the Jew-Gentile problem. His accusers were Jews.

Verses 1-13 are a digression or parenthesis as Paul writes about his ministry to the Gentiles.

Discussion Questions	*Teacher's Commentary and Directives*
Verses 1-13	Verses 1-13
Why was Paul a prisoner? (v. 1).	"For the sake of you Gentiles" (v. 1). It was the animosity of the Jews to his Gentile mission which caused his imprisonment.
What "mystery" or "secret" is Paul writing about which had been hidden to previous generations? (vv. 3-6).	The "mystery" or "secret" is referred to six times in Ephesians.
	"The secret is this: by means of the gospel the Gentiles have a part with the Jews in God's blessings; they are members of the same body, and share in the promise that God made in Christ Jesus" (v. 6).
	The Old Testament prophets and writers knew about salvation for Gentiles but Jews and Gentiles incorporated as fellow members of the body of Christ was a mystery not revealed to them.
Why do you suppose God would call such a strict Jew as Paul to minister to the Gentiles? (v. 7).	*(Teacher, read Acts 9:6, 13-16 for the original call of Paul's ministry to the Gentiles.)*
	Paul's role as a minister was not self-chosen. As a former persecutor of the

Christian believers he felt that he did not deserve such a privilege—it was given to him by "God's special gift which he gave . . . through the working of his power" (v. 7). Undoubtedly the fact that Paul was such a strict Jew had a great effect upon the Gentiles. All of Paul's background—his education, his past experiences—contributed greatly to making him God's special minister.

How does Paul compare himself with God's people?

What is the purpose of Paul's ministry? (v. 8).

"I am less than the least of all God's people" (v. 8; cf. 1 Cor. 15:9; 1 Tim. 1:15).

"To preach to the Gentiles the unsearchable riches of Christ" (NIV) or "the Good News of the infinite riches of Christ" (v. 8).

Here Paul conveys the idea of the things that are most precious being infinitely abundant. Usually precious things are rare. Their rarity increases their price. Here Paul makes us feel that that which is most precious is also boundless and without limit.

What is Paul to make known to all men? (v. 9).

"To make all men see how God's secret plan is to be put into effect."

Paul's first task is to evangelize the Gentiles and at the same time enlighten all mankind as to how the revealed truth meets the needs of men (v. 9).

What was God's purpose in the mystery? (v. 10).

That "by means of the church, the angelic rulers and powers in the heavenly world might know God's wisdom, in all its . . . forms" (v. 10).

100

Discussion Questions	*Teacher's Commentary and Directives*

The Church is now constituted of Jews and Gentiles who have been redeemed by the blood of Christ.

What do you think is meant by the "angelic powers in the heavenly world"? (v. 10).

It is not clear from the text whether only good heavenly beings are meant here, or good and evil. In 6:12, only evil powers are meant by a similar phrase. However, the angels have an interest in the scheme of man's redemption which is referred to in 1 Pet. 1:12. Undoubtedly both good and evil angels are amazed at God's working in redeemed men and women.

What truths are significant in vv. 11 and 12?

God has always planned for man to have an open door to Him. This was accomplished through Christ Jesus (v. 11).

We have no merit of our own through which we can come to God. It is only by union with Christ and through our faith in Him (v. 12).

(Teacher, emphasize to the class the wonderful freedom of access into God's presence which is the privilege of every believer.)

For what reason does Paul exhort his readers to be encouraged? (v. 13).

Paul does not want his readers to be discouraged because of his sufferings. Instead he wants them to feel encouraged and honored because it is for them he is suffering.

(Teacher, for a reference to the severe tribulations which Paul suffered in the vicinity of Ephesus, read 2 Cor. 1:8-11.)

Paul's Prayer for Their Spiritual Growth
(3:14-21)

Paul now returns to the place where he digressed in v. 1. "For this reason" (vv. 1 and 14) to which Paul refers, is found in chapter 2 where he speaks of the extension of divine mercy and saving grace to the Gentiles. The Gentiles now have equal privileges with the Jews through Christ Jesus. Paul's burden in his intercession is that these new believers might experience all the spiritual privileges in their fullness.

Discussion Questions	*Teacher's Commentary and Directives*
Verses 14-19	Verses 14-19
In these opening verses of Paul's prayer, what is his heart attitude in his approach to God? (vv. 14-15).	"I fall on my knees" (v. 14). He approaches God with reverence and holy fear. The Jews usually stood for prayer with outstretched arms to heaven. Here Paul suggests the urgency and the intensity of his prayer.
What are the various petitions of Paul in vv. 16-17?	"To give you power through his Spirit to be strong in your inner selves." ". . . that Christ will make his home in your hearts, through faith." ". . . that you may have your roots and foundations in love." *(Teacher, if the members of your class are new converts, here is an opportunity to explain the second experience of the Christian in which the Holy Spirit cleanses the heart from all sin and empowers the life for service. This experience in the inner man energizes the whole life and enables the new Christian to get his roots down deep in the Christian way.*

Discussion Questions	Teacher's Commentary and Directives

It is the experience which will stabilize the Christian.)

Why is the experience of a Spirit-filled life needed to really understand the love of Christ? (vv. 18-19).

Divine truths are not known by the intellect alone. We cannot know the deep truths of God merely through our human faculties. We need the help of the Holy Spirit (cf. John 14:26; 1 Cor. 2:9-10).

What is the fruit of this knowledge of Christ's love? (v. 19).

That you "be completely filled with the perfect fullness of God" (v. 19).

Though we cannot compare with an infinite God, there may be a correspondence between us. We can enjoy the fullness of grace which God communicates through Christ.

(Teacher, explain that when God saves us He justifies us, He regenerates us, He adopts us into His family. As we walk with Him, the Holy Spirit begins to reveal to us the need for a deeper experience of heart cleansing. As we yield ourselves unreservedly to Him and make a complete consecration of ourselves, He will sanctify us in a crisis experience purifying our hearts by faith and filling us with His Spirit. Cf. Acts 15:8; 1 Thess. 5:23-24.)

Verses 20-21

Study this doxology carefully.

Verses 20-21

In the preceding verses Paul wants the believer to allow God to fill him to capacity. Now he breaks forth in a doxology which declares the greatness of God's power and His glory.

103

Discussion Questions	Teacher's Commentary and Directives
Who is the central person spoken of here and what does Paul ascribe to Him?	Paul speaks of God and His enablement to do what He has promised. There is no limit to God's power. The scope of His power far exceeds the imaginings of the human heart and mind. Paul ascribes the glory to Him. The whole credit for the scheme of grace is due Him. Then Paul links Christ and His Church together: "in the church and in Christ Jesus" (v. 21). This act of adoration is to be done in connection with the work and person of Christ.
Note v. 21, "For all time, forever and ever!" "Throughout all generations, for ever and ever!" (NIV).	This praise to God is not transitory nor will it ever become obsolete or superseded by other views. It is literally "to all the generations" or "the age of the ages."

◆　　◆　　◆

CHAPTER 4

Unity in the Body of Christ

The next three chapters (4—6) of Paul's letter to the Ephesians should teach us how to live the Christian life today. Christianity is a life. Christians are real persons who have been redeemed by a real Savior—Christ Jesus. In the preceding chapters we have had a doctrinal emphasis of the Christian's position in Christ. Now our emphasis is on Christ's living in the Christian.

Discussion Questions	Teacher's Commentary and Directives

Verses 1-16

Verses 1-16

Why do you suppose Paul repeats the fact that he is "a prisoner for the Lord"? (v. 1; cf. 3:1).

Undoubtedly Paul is hoping to provoke his readers to think seriously about their present way of living, for he goes on to exhort them about the way they should live.

What is "the calling" that Paul refers to in v. 1? Is this calling the same for all Christians?

"The calling" which Paul refers to in v. 1 is not a specialized vocation such as a call to the ministry, but it is a gracious invitation for the believer to live in such a way that God is glorified in the new relationship. The call comes to all Christians by the fact that they are Christian.

What are the attitudes Christians should have in their relationships with each other? (vv. 2-3).

Humility, gentleness, patience. Show love by being helpful. "Preserve the unity which the Spirit gives by the peace which binds you together."
(Teacher, emphasize the importance of unity among those in the Body of Christ. Christians need a spirit which stresses more the points in which they agree rather than in which they differ. Those who are divisive, censorious, combative, or careless of peace, do not live a life that measures up to the standard God has set before us.)

What are the seven things listed in vv. 4-6 which are the essence of the Church's oneness?

"One body . . . one Spirit . . . one hope . . . one Lord . . . one faith . . . one baptism . . . one God." These are the fundamentals which form the basis of Christian fellowship in the Church of Jesus Christ.

Why are spiritual gifts not given in equal measure? (v. 7).

Each one in the Body of Christ is given grace or spiritual enablement to "live a life that measures up to the standard

Discussion Questions	Teacher's Commentary and Directives
	God [has] set." The gifts are varied, however, and what each gets he gets for the good of the rest. There is a great variation in human abilities; and gifts are given in the proportion in which the Giver is pleased to give it.
What is meant by verses 8 to 10?	Paul quotes from Ps. 68:18. The point he is making is that Christ as a Conqueror has gifts to distribute to the Church (cf. 1:22).
What are some of the gifts which Paul enumerates? (v. 11).	"Apostles, prophets, evangelists, pastors and teachers." (In 1 Cor. 12:28, Paul has a longer list. However, here he mentions those offices necessary for the growth and nurture of the Church.)
What is the purpose of the gifts? (vv. 12-13).	"To prepare all God's people for the work of Christian service" (v. 12). "To build up the body of Christ" (v. 12). "So we shall all come together to that oneness in our faith and in our knowledge of the Son of God" (v. 13). These verses teach that church unity is strengthened and preserved through the different spiritual gifts of Christian workers in the church. *(Teacher, you may want to discuss the importance of unity in a local Christian congregation and ways to preserve unity.)*
Discuss how we become mature in our Christian experience and reach "the height of Christ's full stature" (v. 13).	Growth comes through prayer, the Word of God, being obedient, and allowing the Holy Spirit to work in our lives. *(Teacher, explain the importance of growth in our Christian experience as individual believers. There can be no*

Discussion Questions	_Teacher's Commentary and Directives_
	growth in the Church apart from our growth as individuals. We must all press toward the fullness of Christ.)
What is an evidence of an immature Christian? (v. 14).	Being able to withstand false doctrine. Those who are unstable in their Christian experience are easily tossed about by "every shifting wind of the teaching of deceitful men" (v. 14). The only adequate safeguard against heresy is a knowledge of the truth and a growing faith in Christ.
What is one of the ways we grow up in Christ? (v. 15).	"By speaking the truth in a spirit of love" (v. 15). The Christian must be genuine himself as an individual as well as speaking the truth. One is not only to speak the truth, but also to live it. Truth must always be connected with love. Love must always be in the disposition and motives.
Note that in v. 16, Paul refers again to the analogy of the body. How does the body develop and what must every part contribute?	Paul uses this analogy to emphasize unity which Christ as the Head brings to the Church. Union to Christ causes growth. The body is to function under His control, in harmony and unity. As the members of the human body help one another to health and maturity by working together, so in the Body of Christ there must be mutual helpfulness.
	Someone defined the Church as an institution that has truth for its nourishment, love for its atmosphere, and Christ for its Head.

107

Exhortation to Break with the Old Life
(4:17—5:20)

We are now in the heart of the practical section of Ephesians. There are many general principles of conduct given as well as practical specifics for daily living. The old and the new life are contrasted; also both the negative and positive aspects of the Christian life are discussed.

Discussion Questions	Teacher's Commentary and Directives
Verses 17-32	**Verses 17-32**
How does Paul describe the way the heathen (Gentiles) live? (vv. 17-19).	"Thoughts are worthless." "Minds are in the dark." "Have no part in the life that God gives, because they are completely ignorant and stubborn" (vv. 17-18). "They have lost all feeling of shame; they give themselves over to vice, and do all sorts of indecent things without restraint" (v. 19). *(Teacher, discuss what is naturally expected of unregenerated people and what they usually give themselves to when they have no capacity for moral or spiritual feeling. Here is an opportunity to point out the clear line of demarcation between the world and the Church. The Christian's way is a contrast to the pagan's life. The Christian must come out from the world and be separate in his manner of life.)*
What has the believer learned of Christ? (vv. 20-21).	"As his followers you were taught the truth that is in Jesus." Here again Paul has a sharp contrast. Note the verses following.

108

Discussion Questions	Teacher's Commentary and Directives
What is contrasted in this paragraph? (vv. 22-24).	Verses 22-24: "The old self and the new self." (In some versions these are referred to as "the old man" and "the new man".) The old self refers to the old, self-centered, self-seeking, corrupt self. The new self or "the new man" is the regenerate self with a new nature in whom Christ is formed.

(Teacher, explain that there is a process of spiritual renewal taking place in those who are in vital union with Christ, but there comes a crisis moment in the experience of entire sanctification when we "put on the new self which is created in God's likeness, and reveals itself in the true life that is upright and holy"—v. 24; cf. Rom. 6:6; 12:1-2). |
| *Discuss the marks of the new life in Christ* (vv. 25-32). | "No more lying" (v. 25). "Do not let . . . anger lead you into sin" (v. 26). "Don't give the Devil a chance" (v. 27). Be honest and upright (v. 28). "Use only helpful words" (v. 29). "Do not make God's Holy Spirit sad" (v. 30). "No more hateful feelings of any sort" (v. 31). "Be kind and tender-hearted to one another" (v. 32). (It is the Holy Spirit who enables us to put away all sinful deeds and gives us the power to live a life that is pleasing to God.) |

CHAPTER 5

A Call to Holy Living

Discussion Questions	Teacher's Commentary and Directives
Verses 1-20	Verses 1-20
In what way is the believer to imitate God? (vv. 1-2).	"Your life must be controlled by love" (v. 2). The Christian walks in the love of Christ which is "shed abroad in our hearts by the Holy Spirit" (Rom. 5:5). We do not achieve divine love by ourselves; it is the gift of God. John says, "Love comes from God. Whoever loves is a child of God and knows God" (1 John 4:7).
What are the sins that are not even to be mentioned among Christians? (vv. 3-4).	"Since you are God's people, it is not right that any questions of immorality, or indecency, or greed should even be mentioned among you. Nor is it fitting for you to use obscene, foolish, or dirty words" (vv. 3-4).
Who will never receive a share in the kingdom of Christ? (v. 5).	"No man who is immoral, indecent, or greedy (for greediness is a form of idol worship) will ever receive a share in the Kingdom of Christ and of God" (v. 5; cf. 1 Cor. 6:9-10). False teachers were arguing that immorality is not a contradiction of the Christian life. The next verses warn us about anyone who may deceive us.

Discussion Questions	Teacher's Commentary and Directives
How does Paul warn us about anyone who may deceive us with foolish words? (vv. 6-7).	"God's wrath will come upon those who do not obey him" (v. 6). "Have nothing at all to do with such people" (v. 7).
What is said of those who are truly God's people? (vv. 8-14).	"You are in the light. So you must live like people who belong to the light." Note the contrasts in these verses. The unsaved person is one in whom the darkness of this world becomes visible.
If the Christian is to have an influence against evil what must he do? (v. 11).	"Have nothing to do with the worthless things that people do, that belong to the darkness. Instead, bring them out to the light" (v. 11). (A life that manifests the light of Christ penetrates the darkness of this world. Conviction comes to the sinful by the very presence of the believer. We are called to awake from the sleep and death of darkness in v. 14 in order that Christ may give us the light of life.)
What exhortations does Paul give regarding the Christian's time? (vv. 15-17).	"Pay close attention to how you live. Don't live like ignorant men . . . Make good use of every opportunity you get . . . Don't be fools, then, but try to find out what the Lord wants you to do." (Time is precious and we must take it seriously by trying to live according to God's will.)
What is the command given in v. 18?	"Be filled with the Spirit" (v. 18). Drunkenness is a work of darkness, those who yield to it act unwisely. Instead of resorting to wine to exhilarate you, Paul says to seek the joy that the Spirit

Discussion Questions	Teacher's Commentary and Directives
	gives you when He comes in His fullness. There is an "inner wine" that fills the soul with songs of gladness, and gives energy for service.
What is an outstanding characteristic of those filled with the Spirit? (v. 20).	Thankfulness and praise to God for everything (v. 20).

Conduct in the Christian Home (5:21—6:9)

Christians owe one another mutual submission as members of the Body of Christ. Paul now devotes much space to the important area of relationships in the home. The biggest test of the gospel's transforming power is in the environment of the home.

Discussion Questions	Teacher's Commentary and Directives
Verses 21-33	Verses 21-33
What does the phrase, "as to the Lord," add to the basic command in v. 22?	Paul is saying that "as it is your duty to be subject to Christ, so also to your husbands." The wife's attitude toward her husband should be one of willing subjection. It is God's plan for the husband to assume the responsibility for the material welfare of the home and also for the spiritual life of the home.
In what sense is the husband the head of the woman? (v. 23).	"The husband is the head of the wife as Christ is the head of the church, his body, of which he is the Savior" (v. 23, NIV). Christ is not an unreasonable taskmaster over His Church, nor a dictator; but He

Discussion Questions	*Teacher's Commentary and Directives*

looks after the interests of the Body. The husband is the protector, guardian, and deliverer of his family.

What should be the husbands' attitude toward their wives? (v. 25).

"Husbands, love your wives in the same way that Christ loved the church and gave his life for it" (v. 25). This is a self-giving love! When there is this kind of unselfish love, there is a loving surrender of the wife in Christian marriage.

Discuss the example Paul gives for husbands to follow (vv. 26-27).

Paul uses the illustration of Christ and the Church (cf. 5:32). Christ gave himself for the Church to "make her holy, cleansing her by the washing with water through the word, and to present her to himself as a radiant church, without stain or wrinkle or any other blemish, but holy and blameless" (vv. 26-27, NIV).

How is a man to love his wife? (vv. 28-29).

"Husbands ought to love their wives as their own bodies" (vv. 28-29, NIV). "He feeds it and takes care of it, just as Christ does the church; for we are members of his body" (vv. 29-30).

Compare v. 31 with Genesis 2:23-24. Discuss the original pattern of marriage suggested as to the closeness of marital bonds.

"For this reason, a man will leave his father and mother, and unite with his wife, and the two will become one" (v. 31), "one flesh" (NIV).

Taken from Adam's side, Eve was actually his flesh and bones. But also being his wife, in a relationship that made the "two . . . one flesh." The union of a Christian husband and wife is to be permanent, intimate, and binding, not marred by divorce.

CHAPTER 6

Children and Parents

Discussion Questions	*Teacher's Commentary and Directives*
Verses 1-4	Verses 1-4
What are the attitudes that are expected of children to their parents? (vv. 1-2).	Obedience and honor (vv 1-2)
What is the promise attached to the commandment in v. 3?	". . . that it may go well with you and that you may enjoy long life on the earth" (v. 3, NIV).
What is the parent's duty negatively and positively in v. 4?	Negatively—"Parents, do not treat your children in such a way as to make them angry" (v. 4). Positively—"Instead, raise them with Christian discipline and instruction" (v. 4). *(Teacher, discuss the importance of a Christian parent as a worker with God, guiding the child to a saving knowledge of Christ. The example of the parent is as indispensable as the precept.)*

Verses 5-9 speak about slaves and masters. The gospel found slavery firmly established in the world. Christianity did not attack slavery outright nor would it have had a chance, being just a tiny Church. But a seed was planted—in Christ slave and master are as one, and the growth of the seed brought social slavery to an end. From this passage some important lessons may be derived as to how Christian employees today can be good witnesses for Christ at their work. Why do many Christians fail to act Christlike on the job at the office or shop? What does this reveal?

Discussion Questions	Teacher's Commentary and Directives
Verses 5-9	**Verses 5-9**
What commands are directed to servants? (vv. 5-8).	"Obey your human masters . . . with a sincere heart, as though you were serving Christ" (v. 5). "Do your work . . . cheerfully" (v. 7). "The Lord will reward every man, whether slave or free, for the good work he does."
What kind of motivation and attitude for masters is given in v. 9?	Masters should have the same attitude toward their slaves. They are not to threaten them. They must remember that there is a Master in heaven "who judges everyone by the same standard" (v. 9). The NIV says: "There is no favoritism with him."

The Christian's Armor (6:10-24)

As we come to the end of Paul's letter to the Ephesians, again we remember that Paul was in prison quarters in Rome as he wrote this passage on the Christian's armor. For over two years Paul had a soldier of the guard attending him night and day. Undoubtedly Paul talked to those soldiers about spiritual matters and perhaps preached this sermon to them first as he observed their armor. Paul recognized that the Christian's conflict is difficult and dangerous, but he also knew that victory is possible through Christ.

Discussion Questions	Teacher's Commentary and Directives
Verses 10-20	**Verses 10-20**
How is the Christian to build up his strength in spiritual warfare? (v. 10).	"In union with the Lord, and by means of his mighty power" (v. 10).
What must every Christian have to be victorious? (v. 11).	"The full armor of God" (v. 11, NIV). Our weapons in this warfare are spiritual. Paul saw in the outfit of the Roman guard the symbols of a supernatural dress for the Christian. (Cf. Rom. 13:12; 1 Thess. 5:8.)
Against whom does the Christian battle? (vv. 11-13).	"We are not fighting against human beings, but against the wicked spiritual forces in the heavenly world." The Christian inevitably engages the opposition of Satan and his hosts, but the Holy Spirit empowers him to resist the attacks. As a Spirit-filled warrior, he must continually strengthen himself with the armor provided for him.
Discuss the Christian's armor. What do the various parts of the armor represent? (vv. 14-17). *Share personal experiences among yourselves to illustrate the truths taught here.*	"Have truth for a belt" (v. 14). "Righteousness for your breastplate" (v. 14). "Readiness to announce the Good News of peace as shoes for your feet" (v. 15). "Faith as a shield" (v. 16). "Salvation for a helmet" (v. 17). "The word of God as the sword" (v. 17).
What does Paul say about prayer? Is prayer related to the armor of	"Do all this in prayer, asking for God's help" (v. 18). "Pray on every occasion" (v. 18).

Discussion Questions	Teacher's Commentary and Directives
the preceding verses?	"Pray always for all God's people" (v. 18). "Pray also for me" (v. 19). ". . . that I may speak boldly" (v. 19). In vv. 18-20 Paul gives a plea for prayer. Prayer is of vital importance for successful warfare, it is the Christian soldier's secret of power.
Verses 21-24 *Who was Tychicus* (vv. 21-22)? *What are the two qualities by which he is noted?*	**Verses 21-24** Tychicus was no doubt the bearer of this letter from Paul to the believers in Asia Minor. Lovableness and faithfulness show that he had much of Paul's own character.
In vv. 23-24 note the four Christian attributes in the concluding benediction.	Verses 23-24: Peace, love, faith, and grace are mentioned in benediction and blessing. Note: Paul began his letter with his favorite word "grace" and ends with the word "grace."

242-7701
Beulah

Susan

KISI - Page 274-2316

CJ- 942-7798

Iowa Head & Neck
274-9135

Dr. stample
255-6320